BRITAIN IN OLD PHOTOGRAPHS

CANTERBURY
REVISITED

DEREK BUTLER

SUTTON PUBLISHING

Sutton Publishing Limited
Phoenix Mill · Thrupp · Stroud
Gloucestershire · GL5 2BU

First published 1997

Reprinted 2004, 2005

Cover photographs: *front*: The front of the Refectory of Blackfriars Monastery, early 1900s; *back*: A Godfrey & Co., pianoforte dealers, cart, early 1900s.

British Library Cataloguing in Publication Data
A catalogue record for this book is available from the British Library.

ISBN 0-7509-1360-6

Typeset in 10/12 Perpetua.
Typesetting and origination by
Sutton Publishing Limited.
Printed in Great Britain by
J.H. Haynes & Co. Ltd, Sparkford.

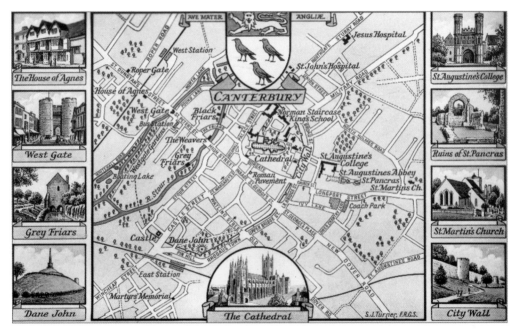

This map postcard was produced in the 1950s and highlights many of the city's historical locations, e.g. St Martin's Church, the Greyfriars, the ruins of St Pancras' Church in the grounds of St Augustine's Abbey and, most important of all, the Cathedral. Above the city's coat of arms can be seen Canterbury's motto 'Ave Mater Angliæ' – 'Hail, Mother of England'.

CONTENTS

The Cathedral Church of Christ towering above the city in a photograph taken in the 1950s. Augustine, the first Archbishop of Canterbury, founded the cathedral (as distinct from the abbey which was later to bear his name) soon after his arrival in 597, and it was hallowed in the name of the 'Holy Saviour'. The original building was gradually enlarged but a series of destructive fires gave Archbishop Lanfranc (1070–93) the opportunity to lay the foundation of the priory church and the building we see today.

INTRODUCTION

Recent figures issued by the English Tourist Board show that visitors to Canterbury Cathedral in 1995 approached the two million mark. In 1997 the city and the Christian Church celebrate the 1,400th anniversary of the arrival of Augustine and his forty monks sent by Pope Gregory. The programme of events will no doubt result in countless more visitors making a pilgrimage to Canterbury which has become the religious capital of the country. The establishment of the first cathedral in England by Augustine a few years after his arrival ensured its place as the Mother Church of the worldwide Anglican Communion and the seat of the Archbishop and Primate of All England. It has also meant that the city of Canterbury has enjoyed a special place in the life and history of the country. Soon after his arrival, Augustine (the first Archbishop of Canterbury) also founded the abbey which now bears his name. It quickly became an important centre of learning as well as the burial place for the Archbishops of Canterbury and the Kings of Kent. The first abbey was completed in the early part of the sixth century and was largely staffed by monks who accompanied Augustine from Rome.

Following the martyrdom of Archbishop Thomas Becket in 1170 the city became an important place of pilgrimage. Many thousands of pilgrims came to pray at his shrine in the Cathedral, a cross-section of which were forever immortalized in Geoffrey Chaucer's *The Canterbury Tales*, written towards the end of the fourteenth century. Most students of English literature will remember the famous words from the General Prologue, 'And specially from every shires ende of Engelond to Caunterbury they wende, The hooly blisful martir for to seke . . .'.

As in earlier selections, many of the picture-postcards in this third book on Canterbury are the work of various photographers who worked in the city over a long period, namely J.G. Charlton, B. & W. Fisk-Moore and Frank Bailey, together with a number of lesser known ones. The debt we owe these photographic artists is enormous – between them they covered all the main events in the life of the city from the 1890s through to the years following the Second World War. The majority of the photographs in this book are from my own collection and these have been supplemented by material loaned by friends and acquaintances who have been pleased to assist in this venture. I have included photographs which particularly appeal to me and am pleased that I have been able to use material relating to the parish of Thanington where I have lived for nearly thirty years. I hope that the selection will bring pleasure not only to the long-standing residents of Canterbury, who will recognize events covered and buildings that are no longer with us, but also to visitors who may be interested to see how the city looked in years gone by. Although the city was irrevocably changed by bombing during the Second World War, development and redevelopment continues to take place and the thousands of visitors who come each year, either from our own country or from abroad (the port of Dover and the Channel Tunnel terminal at Folkestone are only thirty minutes away), will observe a changing scene.

I have endeavoured to obtain copyright permission to reproduce photographs and apologize for any omissions I have made.

The old windmill at Perry Wood was the venue for an outing by the Canterbury Star Cycle Club, 23 July 1911. It was an early type of post mill which ceased working in 1910 and by 1913 had only two sweeps. As it gradually fell into disrepair it became a popular site for picnics and outings, but was finally pulled down in 1920. Sometimes known as Shottenden Mill, it was included in a 1596 map of Kentish windmills and was the subject of a poem by Benjamin Gough in his *Kentish Lyrics* of 1867. The poem is quoted in full in *Watermills and Windmills* (of Kent) written by William Coles Finch, published in 1933, which also recounts how some of the timbers were salvaged by George Reeves of Whitstable. The Star Cycle Club took its name from the old Star Tavern in St George's Place, its headquarters.

EVENTS

The Mayor of Canterbury, the Revd S.G.F. Wilson (third from left) welcoming the Lord Mayor of London to the enthronement service for Dr Cosmo Gordon Lang, the 97th Archbishop of Canterbury, in December 1928.

A number of properties in the High Street were entirely destroyed in a disastrous fire that occurred on 18 August 1865. The fire broke out during the evening in the premises used by John Pout, an upholsterer (at no. 6), and apparently originated in what was once the dormitory of the Chequers of the Hope Inn. Grafton House, the property of draper George Wood (part of the ancient inn), situated on the corner of Mercery lane was affected, but the main damage was done to properties beyond the passage, nos 3 to 9 inclusive, as seen in the photograph.

The devastation caused by the fire in 1865. In his book *Old Canterbury*, Walter Cozens suggests that the fire was caused by 'the upsetting of the pitch pot', but whatever the cause the fire took immediate hold of the buildings and firemen were hard-pressed to control the blaze. The *South Eastern Telegraph* office at no. 3, Jacob Abrahams (glass and china dealer) at no. 4, Mr Colcock (confectioner) at no. 5, Mr Pout at no. 6, George Eastes (piano/music seller) at no. 7 and Sidney Harvey (chemist) at no. 8 all succumbed to the fire. The offices of the *Kent Herald*, at no. 9, were pulled down to prevent the fire spreading to Guildhall Street. All the properties were subsequently rebuilt.

The East Kent Foxhounds meeting at the Barracks under their master, Mr Selby Lowndes, 8 February 1909. The *Kentish Gazette* reported that the weather was ideal and it was not surprised that many hunt devotees proceeded to the starting point (by motor car), although 'a fair number, mostly descendants of the good old yeoman agriculturists proceeded to the start on horseback'.

Members of the East Kent Foxhounds proceeding along the Military Road to their meeting at the Barracks. On the left can be seen part of the old Garrison Church (now called All Saints') and on the right the officers' married quarters. Before the hunt set off at noon in the direction of Trenley Woods they were entertained with 'a sumptuous breakfast in the well-equipped Officers' Mess'.

The Mayor (Francis Bennett-Goldney) together with the Town Clerk, Henry Fielding, during the proclamation procession around the city on 9 May 1910. The Mayor's carriage is seen passing along Lower Bridge Street with the home of James Reid, FRCS (no. 12) in the background. Dr Reid served the Kent and Canterbury Hospital from 1846 to 1911 as an honorary and consulting surgeon. The buildings seen here were destroyed in the 1942 blitz.

The carnival entry of the Canterbury Master Bakers, August 1910. The front of the float featured a revolving windmill and on board were Messrs Newing, Kay, Webb, Saunders, Read and Joad, all dressed in their white overalls. Their entry won first prize for the best trade car. In the previous year their entry failed to make the start of the carnival after the horses were startled and the float wrecked.

The custom of 'Beating the Bounds' was carried out from time to time in the early years of the twentieth century. This 1910 photograph by J.G. Charlton shows Francis Bennett-Goldney, the Mayor (with the white scarf) and others in the party crossing the River Stour on the boundary between the city and the parish of Sturry at Providence Place, Sturry Road. One or two in the boat look rather apprehensive as they are towed across the river.

Morris men taking part in the celebrations marking the visit of the Chief Scout, Lord Baden Powell, in September 1930. After receiving the Freedom of the City he went on to the Victoria Recreation Ground to be welcomed by 6,000 cheering scouts and guides. The display of morris dancing was given by the 4th Sevenoaks Rovers; gymnastics, bridge-building and a camp-fire singsong were also on the programme arranged by District Commissioner S.E. Haynes and Alderman G. Barrett.

St Peter's Place, a quiet cul-de-sac that was prone to flooding from the River Stour. In October 1909 many streets in the Westgate area of the city were flooded and St Peter's Place was no exception. Holy Cross and St Peter's School was located at the end of the road and the notice on the right, 'Schools Closed', summed up the situation. St Peter's Place is now one of the busiest roads into the city.

North Lane during the severe floods of 1909, when the city suffered 4 in of rain over a three-day period. The photograph shows a horse and cart from the coal merchants Pilch Collard & Co. Ltd. heading toward the Westgate. The attractive old cottages on the left and the weatherboarded dwellings on the right have long disappeared. Quite a number of other properties in the lane were also lost in the last war owing to enemy action.

A carnival float with a nautical flavour dating from the early 1930s. James Powell of Palace Street took this photograph of *Zora Star* at the assembly point in Littlebourne Road. The crew were ready with their collecting boxes for the Mayor's New Hospital Appeal. 'Please help to build the New Hospital' was the message on the boxes. The new Kent and Canterbury Hospital was officially opened in July 1937.

'The Hospital Collecting Pack' was the name of this carnival entry in the 1930s. During these years appeals relating to the new Kent and Canterbury Hospital had a high profile and this particular one was for the Mayor's appeal for the Maintenance Fund. This Fisk-Moore photograph features some of the nurses from the hospital.

A pageant procession making its way up Broad Street in August 1924. The properties on the right of the photograph (down as far as the white-painted Brewer's Delight public house just beyond the car) were all casualties of the 1942 bombing. Historic events in the history of the city were depicted in the pageant, which was organized by the City Social Guild in aid of local charities.

'Miss Canterbury' in 1973 was young Carole Mace. Carole is seen here holding her trophy with attendants Christina Wyatt (on her right) and Susan Miles. The carnival was organized by a sub-committee of the council under the chairmanship of Councillor Archie Stoakes and was held after a break of six years. The mammoth procession featured thirteen Beauty Queens and eight bands in the grand total of seventy-seven floats. (Reproduced with permission of Kent Messenger Group Newspapers)

The City Council processing to the old Guildhall during the Mayoralty of Mrs Evelyn M. Hews, which lasted from November 1946 to May 1949. The Town Sergeant, Edward Roberts, carrying the Mace, precedes the Mayor and Town Clerk, John Boyle. Controversy still marks the decision to demolish the medieval Guildhall in 1950 after it was found to be unsafe. The cost of renovation was considered to be too high at the time.

John Marsh leading a contingent of the Royal Air Force Association in a parade marking Battle of Britain Sunday in 1969. Taking the Salute is the Mayor, Herbert Buckworth, supported by the Sheriff, Bernard Porter. The rostrum is set up in the entrance to the Longmarket, which was redeveloped in the late 1950s, the second occasion since the last war. Murdoch's radio and television shop can be seen in the background with the baker's shop of Nicholas Kingsman to its right.

An aerial view of the fire at Abbot's (or Denne's) Mill which destroyed it completely, 17 October 1933. After the Cathedral the mill was the next best-known location in the city and was built in 1792 as the city granary to a design by John Smeaton. The extent of the fire shows how vulnerable the houses in St Radigund's Street, Abbot's Place and Mill Lane were, especially the Miller's Arms public house. The Canterbury Municipal Fire Brigade was first to tackle the fire and was later joined by brigades from Bridge, Sturry and Herne Bay. The alarm was given at about 8.30 a.m. that a fire had broken out in the hay loft and the mill was soon a raging inferno. Within about three hours the six-storey timber building was reduced to ashes. Firemen can be seen fighting the fire from the bridge over the River Stour and onlookers standing in St Radigund's Street to the left of the bridge (centre of the photograph).

The official openning of the Westgate Gardens by the Mayor, Charles Lefevre, 1937. Also in the picture are, left to right, Mrs Lefevre, Mrs Catherine Williamson and Mr Stephen Williamson. Tower House and grounds comprising 11 acres were donated to the city by the Williamson family, and are preserved by deed for the benefit of the citizens. Catherine Williamson followed in the steps of Charles Lefevre by becoming Mayor in 1938 and 1939.

A vehicle used by William Lefevre Ltd. decorated for a carnival entry in the 1930s. William Lefevre and his wife came to the city in 1875 (his father originally had a greengrocer's shop in Military Road) and set up their draper's shop in Sun Street. William and Frances Lefevre had fifteen children, the youngest of whom, Charles, took over the business and became one of the city's most illustrious citizens.

The Exeter public house at 57 Broad Street, *c.* 1921. Regulars of the inn are shown with their highly decorated carnival entry; Elizabeth Chapman, the licensee's wife can be seen on the right (in the white dress) and her son, Fred, in the front of the wagon, which was borrowed from Pickfords. Billy King is standing beside the horse and Arthur Hadson in front of the wagon. The Exeter was a free house with all 'local beers drawn from the wood'. It closed just before the last war. Mrs Chapman later became licensee of the Woodman's Arms in Wincheap.

Regulars from the Cross Keys public house on an outing in the late 1920s, visiting a Shepherd Neame inn somewhere in East Kent. Among those in the photograph are Richard Monk, licensee of the Cross Keys for over thirty-five years, 'Chalky' Smith, Joe Wright, Henry Ticehurst, William Everton, members of the Small family, 'Pasha' Baker, Alec (later Sir Alec) Rose, who sailed single-handed around the world in 1967–8, Chas, 'Chippy' Norton, Bill Cook, Wally Wiffen and Alf Hogbin.

Artillery Street celebrated the Silver Jubilee of King George V's reign in fine style, 6 May 1935. Many local families turned out for this photograph with their banner proclaiming 'Poor but Loyal' and 'Long Live the King'. Quite a number of those seen here would appear in a similar and more famous photograph published in the *Kent Messenger* following the VE Day celebrations ten years later. The old houses in the street were demolished in 1962 prior to redevelopment.

The King and Queen chatting to the King's School Captain, A.A. Kneller, on their visit in 1946. The Captain welcomed Their Majesties with a Latin oration, a translation of which was printed in the *Kentish Gazette* of 13 July – presumably the King had already seen the English version. The Queen apparently asked Mr Kneller if the oration had been arduous for him – he agreed it had been as it had taken him four weeks to learn, adding that Latin was not his strong subject!

King George VI and Queen Elizabeth visited the city in July 1946 and the smiling King can be seen
touching the scabbard of the city's ancient sword held by the Mayor, Alfred Baynton. This ceremony took
place by the Westgate Towers and denoted the fact that the King accepted the city's homage. The King,
Queen and Princess Elizabeth had travelled by train to Selling and on to Canterbury by car and in the
words of the *Kentish Gazette* were given a 'tumultuous welcome'. Alfred Baynton, who was the city's
Sheriff in 1934, joined the newly formed East Kent Road Car Co. Ltd. as its first secretary in 1916 and
was General Manager from 1942 until he retired in 1948.

Field Marshal Bernard Montgomery visiting Canterbury in October 1945 to receive the Freedom of the City. He was welcomed at the Westgate by the Deputy Mayor, Councillor J.H.B. Young, the Sheriff, Councillor J.G.B. Stone, the Town Clerk, John Boyle and Town Sergeant Lilley, who can all be seen in the photograph. 'Monty' inspected a Guard of Honour from the Royal Warwickshires, his old regiment, in St Dunstan's Street. Along with many other children, I, together with my family, was in this large crowd which welcomed one of the Second World War heroes to the city. The shops on the left include W. & R. Fletcher Ltd. (butchers), the County Laundry and Sidney Terry Ltd. (electrical contractors).

The VE party for Ashford Road children held in the field behind Mr Elvidge's house, May 1945. Among those identified are Mrs Day, Mr Henley and members of the following families: Burroughs, Elvidge, Filby, Flanders, Jennings, Lewry, Page, Percival, Pilcher, Rampley, Roberts, Swain, Tinsley, Wadsworth, White and Vidler. The oldest surviving member of the group is Fred Kemp (extreme right) now in his ninetieth year.

Members of the Thanington Without Women's Institute photographed on a visit to Lullingstone, 1953. The party includes, sitting down (left to right): Mrs Griffiths and Elizabeth, Mrs Palmer, Mrs Evans, Mrs Chynoweth, Mrs Thompson, Mrs Bradshaw, Miss Pine with Jill and Mrs Page with David; standing: Mrs Smithson-Birch, Mrs Blissett, Mrs Ralph, Mrs Sanders, Mrs Corbett, Mrs Edwards, Mrs Ashenden, Mrs Sample, Mrs King, Mrs Fagg, Mrs Lillywhite, Mrs Askem, Mrs Mitchell, Miss Pine, Mrs Reynard, Mrs Skinner, Mrs Newbery, Mrs Day and Miss Audrey Dale.

Employees and their families of Finn & Co. pictured outside the Imperial Hotel, Martyr's Field Road. The photograph dates from just after the First World War and the group were off on an outing in Finn's Thornycroft lorry. Finn & Co. were Engineers and Contractors and had a depot at Seymour Place, Wincheap. Standing by the cab (with bow tie) was the driver William Beale – his future wife Winifred Best can be seen in the cab.

An outing from the Tally Ho public house in Clyde Street, *c.* 1946. Those standing include Tom Ellis, Fred Neves, Bert Tucker, Joe Duncan, Ernie Baldock, Arthur Denny, Jack Allen, Andy Gallagher, Bert Smith, Stan Burrows, Jimmy Long, Ned Norris, Alf Osmond, Arthur Lane and Bill Horton. Those on the coach include Hilda Smith, Les Todd, Henry Routen, Ted Edwards, Jack Bushell and Bill Allen.

The St John Ambulance Brigade photographed at the Simon Langton Schools, in 1929. The two officers in the centre of the front row are C.T. Richardson on the left and C.C. Elam, the Treasurer. Mr Elam, known as 'Boss', taught at the school for many years and will be remembered by many older Langtonians. Other personnel identified in the picture are Messrs Cox, Lye, Robins, Briggs, Terry, Coultham, Wells and Shelley, the Hon. Secretary, sitting on Mr Elam's left.

Members of the Thanington (No. 2 Division) St John Ambulance Brigade which was formed in February 1936. This photograph was taken at Hollow Lane and includes Major H.S. Hardy (centre of back row) from Thanington Court, the Honorary Treasurer, and the Rector, the Revd V.T. Macy, President. The group, to which quite a number of local coalminers belonged, also includes L/Corp. J. Amess and Messrs Parker, H. Lye and R. Mitchell.

INNS, RESTAURANTS
& SHOPS

The Cross Keys public house in Oaten Hill in the 1950s, when it also incorporated Kingsfield's bakery on the left (numbered in Old Dover Road). In the early 1960s the shop was taken over by Martin's electrical business but is now part of the seventeenth-century Cross Keys.

The Sign of Dover public house in Old Dover Road in the early twentieth century. Situated next door to Ye Old Forge House, the inn closed in the First World War and became a private dwelling in 1927, when it was renamed Sundial House. As well as having a public telephone, the inn was also a 'receiving' office for A.W. Anderson's omnibuses and cabs. Nearly opposite the inn stood St Lawrence Mill, a Black Stock Mill, which burnt down in the spring of 1873.

Billy White (William Francis White) was proprietor of the Oporto Tavern in St Peter's Street from the mid-1930s to the 1950s. This cartoon of 'Mine Host' was produced as a postcard and given away to customers. The Oporto Tavern closed in 1969 and the premises are now a shop called Welby's Bazaar, named after former owners Welby & Co., wine and spirit merchants.

The Mitre Inn situated in the Friars, in the late 1940s. Standing almost opposite the Marlowe Theatre it changed its name to Canterbury Tales in 1981. To the left of it can be seen the old store belonging to the long-established ironmongers Field & Jordan – John Field was actually trading in St Peter's Street in the 1870s. The store was demolished some years ago.

The Hop Poles public house at 107 Wincheap, in the late 1940s when owned by Mackeson. Situated very close to an oast house and not far away from Lillywhite's hop gardens, the property was extended in about 1950 when the building on the left (the old Thanington Dairy) was demolished. The Hop Poles was rebuilt in the early part of the twentieth century.

Gaywood's Canterbury Restaurant at 41 High Street in the 1930s. It could seat 200 and was a popular venue for wedding receptions and parties, etc. Its attractive interior can be seen in this picture, when it had been taken over by James Long of the Savoy Café Restaurant. After the last war the rooms upstairs were used for a time by the Sidney Woodman School of Dancing and from the mid-1950s by Hugh Connolly, a dance teacher.

The Savoy Café Restaurant at 9 High Street showing its attractive interior in the 1920s. James Long took over the restaurant from Francis Pololi at the beginning of the First World War (when luncheons cost 1s. and afternoon teas started at 5d.) and continued until the late 1940s by which time Mr Long had opened his establishment in Church Street St Paul's. This photograph shows part of the restaurant which could seat 160 persons. After the last war Blindell's shoe shop occupied the premises.

The Dutch Tea House at 24 St Peter's Street commenced trading during the First World War. At that time luncheons cost 1*s*. 6*d*. and a few years later you could listen to music between 4 p.m. and 6 p.m. daily. This photograph, taken in the 1930s, shows part of the comfortable interior of the tea house, which was a popular venue for local people. The 'Dutch' continued in business until the late 1950s; it stood adjacent to the old Sidney Cooper School of Art.

The 11th Century Tea Rooms in Church Street St Paul's in the late 1950s. A. & D. Rose had taken over from James Long & Co. by this time. An article in the *Kent County Journal* of 1949 commented that 'the bakery, shop and restaurant are housed in an ancient building with attractive timbering inside, and a projecting upper storey which proclaims its antiquity to those who approach it for the first time'.

St Dunstan's Café, located at the junction of St Dunstan's Street and Westgate Grove, 1930s. This photograph shows the property with a mock-Tudor façade. After the last war the property on the corner became Ben Lee's antique shop which remained until the 1980s when it returned to being a café. The row of houses in the Grove facing the river mostly date from the 1600s. In the late 1930s the establishment was known as the Riverside Hotel and Café.

William Peters' St Dunstan's Restaurant at 82 St Dunstan's Street featured on a postcard posted in June 1906. Mr Peters was also a baker and confectioner and the business was known as the Model Bakery by the 1920s. On the left can be seen part of H.W. Bateman's premises (builder and undertaker). Mr Bateman subsequently took over no. 82 in about 1930. Both premises are now hairdressing salons.

Edwin R. Biggleston was in business as a dispensing chemist at 11 Mercery Lane in the early 1890s and carried on until the First World War. Edwin was the son of William Biggleston who set up an Iron and Brass Founder's business with J.G. Drury in 1835. The story of *The Bigglestons of Canterbury* has recently been published by the Local History Group of the Oaten Hill and District Society.

Burniston & Co. coal and coke merchant's business, 1928. This business was situated at 2 Guildhall Street from the beginning of the twentieth century through to the 1940s when P. Hawksfield took over. The manager is seen posing in the doorway. One of the posters in the window offers a shilling discount per ton for cash. The shop was next door to the old Congregational Church.

Frederick Charles Snell's first shop was at 7 Guildhall Street and he was in business by 1893. Mr Snell was a picture framer and sold fancy goods and toys etc. This early twentieth-century photograph shows the window crammed with goods and possibly features Mrs Snell standing in the doorway. In the early 1900s the business expanded into the adjoining property, no. 8, and this concentrated on toys and fancy goods. These shops were situated just along from Ben Jonson Inn (no. 10) with Nye's Oyster rooms at no. 9. All these shops were taken over by William Lefevre Ltd. after the First World War and incorporated into their store (now Debenhams).

F.C. Snell's shop at 46 St Peter's Street in the early 1930s. Mr Snell transferred his picture framing business to this address after the First World War and continued trading until the late 1930s. After the last war the property was used by grocers, World Stores Ltd. Mr Snell was responsible for a fascinating book entitled *The Intermittent (or Nailbourne) Streams of East Kent* which was printed and published by Hunt, Snell & Co. in 1937.

Walter Hunt established his stationer's business at 41 Palace Street over a hundred years ago and this photograph dates from about 1897. The premises were part of the large gatehouse to the Archbishop's Palace built in the 1560s. Among the books in the attractive window display (decorated for a competition) is a copy of *The Nansen North Pole Picture Book* priced at 1s. together with toys, games and a selection of china items manufactured by W.H. Goss.

The tailor's shop of Ernest Geeson located at The White House, 21c Burgate Street, *c.* 1912. 'Tailoring that fits the purse and person' and 'Everything a man wants' were two of the advertisements on the front of the shop, with trousers at 4*s*. 11*d*. and ready to wear suits at 18*s*. 6*d*! Before moving to these premises in about 1910–11, Mr Geeson had a shop at no. 44 (The Red House) on the corner of Butchery Lane.

Mr Geeson's advertising postcard gave details of his trading philosophy – money back if you were not satisfied. The White House was situated opposite the entrance to Longmarket (or Corn and Hop Exchange). It was destroyed by enemy action in 1942, a few years after Ernest Geeson ceased trading. The postcard was addressed to 'U.R. Sure, 2 Want a Suit, So Oblige, By Reading'!

FROM ⌒

GEESON'S, the White House, Burgate St., Canterbury

(Facing the Market).

WE ARE THE MONEY-BACK CLOTHIERS!

That is to say, if you purchase a Suit of us, and it is not entirely satisfactory, you bring back the Suit (not worn), and we return you your money.

WE CAN AFFORD TO MAKE THIS OFFER,

1st—Because we hardly ever hear of a Suit being unsatisfactory.

2nd — Because an offer like this begets the confidence of the public.

THAT SUIT YOU WILL NEED SHORTLY,

You want to KNOW that it will *fit*, that it will *wear*. Purchase it at the " WHITE HOUSE." It will pay us to make it satisfactory in every detail ; if not, we are the losers—you lose nothing !

OUR SUITS TO MEASURE are

Smarter and better fitting than ever. Our New Patterns are A1. Prices—25/6 to 70/-

OUR READY-TO-WEAR SUITS

Fit so well that you could not detect them as being " Ready-Made." Prices—18/6 to 35/-

GEESON The White House, (*facing the*) Burgate St., Canterbury (*Market.*)

West & Son, Drapers and Milliners, *c.* 1910.
This J.G. Charlton photograph shows their
premises at 8/9 The Parade, on the corner of St
Margaret's Street. The business was established
before 1878 and survived until the First World
War. The fourth storey gable and the attic on
the extreme right can still be seen but the
ornamental lamppost and the chimney stack on
West's have disappeared. This late medieval
building was probably once used to house
pilgrims.

Jay's Furnishing Stores moved to 1 Guildhall
Street after the blitz in 1942, when their
premises at Marlowe House (57/58 St
George's Street) were destroyed. Jay's
established their business at St George's Street
(at the junction with St George's Lane) in the
1930s but it was not until the early 1950s that
they were able to return there (at no. 32)
following the redevelopment. Part of the
Seven Stars Hotel at 1 Orange Street can be
seen on the right.

The greengrocer's shop of Mary Ann Tuff, 3 Dover Street, 1880s. Presumably the people outside are customers though the gentleman in the doorway looks a bit more important, and could be Mr Tuff. At that time no. 2 (on the right) was the premises of Albert Neame, a wood turner. The photograph was published by F. W. Nichols of 18 St George's Terrace.

The tobacconist's shop of Percy W. Parsons at 3 Dover Street, photographed by Mr Parsons after the last war. Part of 4 Dover Street can be seen on the left – the newsagent's shop of Edward Carr with its advertisements for 'Lilliput' and 'John Bull' above the window. Mr Parsons, a keen photographer, started his business after the First World War. It did not cease until the late 1960s, having been looked after for many years by Mrs Parsons.

Henry Bear's Grocery Stores at 107 (old numbering) Wincheap Street, before the First World War. Mr Bear took over the shop in the early 1900s and the business continued, with his son, into the early 1950s when it was taken over by S.J. Kilby Ltd. The premises, adjacent to the old St Mildred's Hall, remained a grocer's until the 1980s and is now a fish and chip restaurant, now 33 Wincheap Street.

F.J. Clayson's shop at 27 Wincheap, 1931. Frederick Clayson established his business as a watchmaker and jeweller in 1908. His son subsequently took over the business which continued trading until the late 1970s. It is likely that the photograph shows Mr Clayson's son with his pedal car. The premises are now used by Cico Stoves and Chimneys Ltd.

The Hairdressing Saloon of Charles Greenstreet at 16 Palace Street in the 1960s. Mr Greenstreet took over his father's old business after the First World War and continued trading until the 1970s. The property dates from the eighteenth century and was formerly the Albion public house which closed before 1908. It is said that the Albion had a somewhat doubtful reputation!

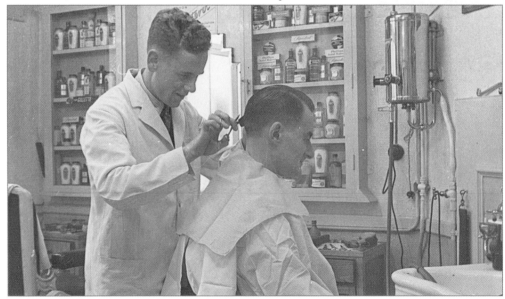

This photograph shows the interior of the Hairdressing Saloon with Tommy Lennox cutting Charles Greenstreet's hair. I was a regular client in the 1950s and as a teenager can remember being addressed as 'Sir' by Mr Greenstreet! Tommy Lennox was the assistant hairdresser from 1948 to 1966 and was the only person trusted by Mr Greenstreet to cut his hair. A number of Brylcreem products can be seen in the cabinets.

Vera and Bert Cole's hairdressing business at 3 and 4 The Borough, 1939. They established their business in 1935 – Mrs Cole's salon was called 'Maison Coiffures' and Mr Cole looked after the gentlemen next door, ably assisted by Lou Howard, Mr Cole's first apprentice. Lou is seen here (on the left) with Bert outside the shop. Lou Howard retired in 1983 after forty-eight years at the shop, broken only by wartime service with the Royal Artillery in Burma. I was a customer at Cole's in the 1960s and 1970s and can testify to the skill and patience of the staff. It was a popular establishment and at lunchtimes you could wait a long time for your turn in the chair. Bert Cole died in 1978 but the business continued with the family until a few years ago. The photograph also shows the tile-hung façades on the pair of timber-framed buildings and part of the old baker's shop of Frank Baylis on the extreme right.

Tony Wright standing in the doorway of his Stamp Shop at 29 Palace Street in Coronation Year, 1953. Mr Wright started his shop business in 1946 and carried on trading for nearly thirty years. As well as the shop there was a postal business which had been established many years before. In the 1950s the old cycle shop of Albert Anderson at no. 30 was taken over as the business expanded to include stationery, greetings cards, jokes and novelties, etc.

By the late 1960s Wright's Stamp Shop had extended to no. 32 where Mrs Jarrett had previously had a fruit shop. In the various departments Tony was assisted by his wife, Nina, and his mother-in-law, Mrs Wells. The eighteenth-century buildings, numbered 29 to 31 Palace Street, seen here, relate to the properties numbered within the Borough on the opposite side of the road. The shop windows still remain today, although the shutters around the single window have been removed. Mr and Mrs Wright have been retired for some years, but still take a keen interest in philately.

Bill Rigden, manager of the greengrocery department at David Greig's 'temporary' shop at 19/21 Sun Street, c. 1948. This was opened within a week or so of their premises at 12 and 13 St George's Street being destroyed by enemy action in June 1942. David Greig remained in Sun Street until their new shop was opened at 23 St George's Street in 1953.

The ironmonger's shop of Henry Ovenden at 31 Burgate Street, in the late 1920s. The staff in the white coats are Vic Ovenden (on the left) and Bill Blackman, On display is a varied selection of galvanized buckets and watering cans as well as a number of lawn mowers. The Ovenden family was in business in Burgate from the 1880s until the late 1950s when Alfred Olby Ltd. took over the premises.

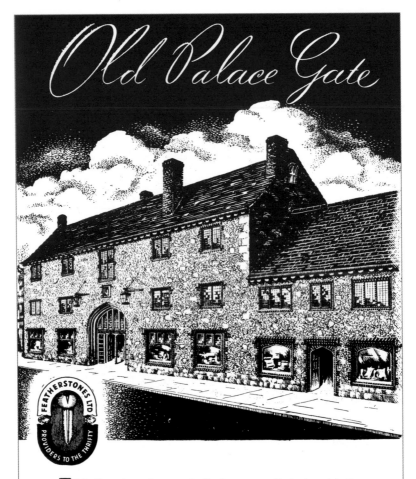

Featherstones Ltd. opened their stores at the Old Palace Gate in 1927 occupying 41–43 Palace Street. They expanded into the two-storey building to the right, no. 44, after the Second World War. A medieval building, the gatehouse of the Archbishop's Palace was restored earlier in this century and is faced with flint and stone. In 1957 Featherstones moved to new premises in Burgate Street where they remained until the store closed in 1970. The King's School took over the Palace Street premises when Featherstones left. In the 1890s and early 1900s Walter Hunt the stationer occupied no. 41, with nos 42 and 43 used by Gibbs & Sons the printers. Featherstones' advertising in the 1930s reminded customers that they were 'Head to Foot Outfitters and General Providers to the Thrifty'. The doorway in the two-storey building has now been replaced by a window.

HOP PICKING &
COMMERCIAL LIFE

A toddler in a local hop garden surveys the scene from the safety of a tally basket, c. 1940. The remains of the picked bines can be seen stacked at the side of each alley.

W. Hubble & Sons' hop gardens at Harbledown with the farm workers standing by the loaded sacks ready for transporting to the oast houses for drying. The large sacks (or pokes) could accommodate two tallies' worth of hops, the equivalent of ten bushels. Tally baskets, which could take five bushels, can be seen at the end of the row (or alley), each basket holder having their own number. This was one of a series of photographs taken by Frank Bailey in 1930.

A happy group of hop pickers and farm workers pose for Frank Bailey's camera in the Harbledown hop gardens. The tally basket into which the pickers have emptied their various boxes, baskets and tin baths, etc. is about to be poured into a large sack held by the farm workers. The farm bailiff (possibly a Mr Ash), standing on the left wearing a hat, noted the amount picked by each basket holder in an account book.

A family picking in bushel baskets in Hubble's hop gardens. The full baskets in the foreground are topped up with a 'head' on them to allow the hops to settle at a full bushel measure. The farm worker on the right has a large pole which was used for bringing down parts of the bines missed by the pickers. He was known as the pole puller or binman, though it was only in West Kent that large bins were used by pickers.

A tally basket of hops being emptied into a sack in Wacher's hop gardens at Stuppington Lane, 1930s. This is a typical hop garden scene with an array of baskets and tin baths for picking in and discarded bines which have been picked. After a long hot September's day picking (as a child I recall that there were many interesting things to do in and around the hop gardens!) it was a relief to hear the binman call out 'pull no more bines', a signal to start clearing up.

A series of photographs taken by Percy Parsons in Blake Wacher's hop gardens at Stuppington Lane in the 1930s, showing a tally man at work. In the top left picture the tally man can be seen with a set of tallies around his waist – pieces of wood which could be marked with the amount of hops collected. The one below shows the picker pouring her hops carefully into the tally basket so that none were spilt on to the ground. The bottom right picture shows the tally basket being emptied into a sack for removal to the oast house. The top right picture completes the sequence with the tally man sorting out his tallies after measuring the hops. Hop pickers were subject to a number of rules and regulations such as to 'pick the hops well to the employer's satisfaction . . . to pick up all dropped hops and to have their hops ready for the measurer so that no delay may arise'. No hops could be picked during the official dinnertime and 'no spiritous liquor [was] to be bought or sold in the hop gardens; no abusive or immoral language [was] to be made use of and no fighting or quarrelling [was] to take place'. Such were the joys of hop picking that many local families were involved in before machines took over in the early 1970s.

Henry Ellenor had his carriage-building works in Best Lane, just behind the old Gospel Mission Room. He was in business there in the early 1890s and continued until the end of the First World War. Among the staff seen here are Francis Biggs (centre of front row), holding a rasp, and his son Ted (on his left), with a large hammer. After the Second World War the premises became the cathedral's stained glass department. The wagon on the right belonged to Johnson & Co. of the Northgate Brewery.

George Shilling (on the left) in his forge at 5 Best Lane. Mr Shilling set up his blacksmith's business after the First World War and continued in business in Best Lane until the late 1940s. Mr Shilling was responsible for repairing the ancient ironwork used to house the stained glass in the Cathedral. The site of the old forge has now been redeveloped.

Staff posing by their machines at the printing works of Walter Hunt at 41 Palace Street in the 1890s. Posters on the wall refer to Queen Victoria's Diamond Jubilee in 1897. The business continued with John W. Hunt who for many years traded at 'Calendar House', 18 St Margaret's Street and subsequently became Hunt, Snell & Co. The latter's premises were destroyed in the Baedeker raid on 1 June 1942.

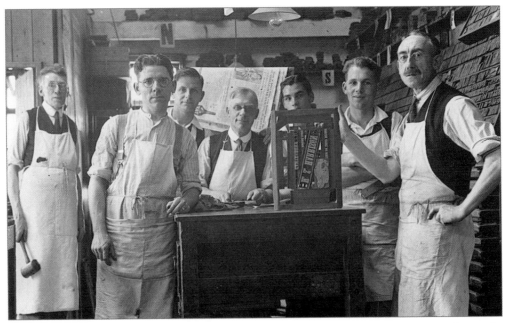

A group of local employees pose for the camera in the printing works of a local newspaper during the 1930s. One of the advertisements being set is for H.S. Harrison, Oyster and Lobster Merchant of 6 Butchery Lane. It is interesting to note that Mr Harrison was in business (at 5 Guildhall Street) as early as 1878 and continued until about 1940 in Butchery Lane.

The steam lorry of W. Hooker & Son of Westgate Mill in the 1920s. 'Our Self-Raising Flour is "Ideal"' was the slogan on the side of the vehicle which was manufactured by the Sentinel Waggon Works at Shrewsbury. The vehicle had a speed limit of 12 m.p.h., or just 5 m.p.h. with a trailer. Westgate Mill was acquired by W. Hooker from T.S. Cooper in 1891.

A Sentinel steam lorry belonging to Kingsford & Co. of Barton Mills, Sturry Road. late 1920s. This Sentinel DG6, with a closed body, is seen here before its delivery to Kingsfords. 'Aurora' was the name of the self-raising flour produced by the millers. It is interesting to note that William Kingsford was milling in the city during the latter part of the eighteenth century.

Farmers closely inspecting the tethered cattle at the cattle market, in the late 1930s. Onlookers standing behind the railings on St George's Terrace had a very good view of the proceedings. The building on the left was used by the Halifax Building Society. The adjoining ivy-clad Sun Building stood on the corner of the Terrace and St George's Street. The large building in the centre was Martin's the drapers.

An advertising postcard sent out by Walter Hogben of 35 Broad Street relating to the hire of marquees and tents. Mr Hogben also ran a tobacconist's business at this address from the 1890s until the First World War. The card was sent on 3 November 1904 to a local client and was signed 'Yours obediently'. The photograph was taken by George Thompson who had his studio at 70 Northgate.

The cattle market on a busy day, 1936. Young and old alike seem fascinated by the scene below them as farmers inspect the livestock. The photographer was looking towards Lower Bridge Street when taking this shot and two East Kent buses can be seen passing each other at the entrance to St George's Place. The trees on the Upper Bridge Street side of the market made it an attractive site. In the sixteenth century nearby Dover Street was called Ritherchiape (meaning 'cattle market') and there is no doubt that the cattle market operated in this immediate area for over a thousand years until it transferred to a new site in 1955. The old market was given over to car parking (this was extremely useful for patrons of the nearby Regal cinema) until the second stage of the ring road came about in 1969. In 1934 the City Council and local farmers were at odds over the council's proposal to move the market to the St Stephen's area. The *Kentish Gazette* of 22 March reported that 'the rank and file of farmers and auctioneers still hope that the site on the junction of three railways at Whitehall will eventually be adopted, because when the Northern by-pass road is constructed it will pass the top end of the market area and provide both easy access from Ashford, Maidstone, etc. and an outlet to Thanet'.

Arthur Bell's bookbinding business at 3 and 4 Butchery Lane in the 1920s. It was originally located at 8 St Peter's Grove, but moved to Butchery Lane in the early twentieth century. The 'City Bindery' which is seen here provided services including bookbinding, account book manufacture and machine ruling. The business remained in Butchery Lane until it became part of Canterbury Printers in the 1970s and moved to Hall Place, Harbledown.

The firm of Godfrey & Co., pianoforte dealers, had their premises at 2 St George's Gate from the early 1900s. As can be seen from the cart, they had other branches in Kent as well as in London, across the South coast and as far west as Exeter. This pre-First World War photograph shows 'Taff' the horse outside a local blacksmith's. Godfrey & Co. carried on their business in the city until the early 1920s.

The Canterbury Electric Welding Co., 20 Roper Road, *c.* 1930. This business was set up by John Vissenga in the early 1920s. Roper Road was developed in about 1890 and was originally called Hanover Place. The welding business carried on until the late 1950s. John Vissenga was an enthusiastic photographer and produced a number of cine-films of local events during the 1930s.

The staff at Cadbury Bros. depot, 1932. Cadbury's premises were in Station Road East, now occupied by a snooker club. Those shown are, back row (left to right): Bob Lucas, Jimmy Creaby, Fred Kennett, -?-, Layton Dawes; middle row: -?-, Joan Hills, Gwen Bartlett, Erica Stockwell, Rita Millington, Win Cox, Fred Smith; front row: Bill Hughes, Nellie Roberts, Albert Bailey (manager), Jack Straw, Monica Hall and Norman Ackroyd.

An East Kent bus (a Tilling Stevens TS3) being filled with coal gas during the last years of the First World War. With petrol rationed a number of vehicles were adapted to run on gas which was stored in a collapsible bag on the roof. These bags were rather fragile and it was reported that some blew off buses travelling between Folkestone and Dover. This vehicle is outside the Gas and Water Company's premises in Castle Street.

Aerial view of the South Coast Concrete Co. in the 1930s. Their works were established between Milton Bridge and Chartham in the late 1920s. The company was owned by Wm. Griffiths & Co. Ltd. and their site covered fifteen acres. Their claim that they stocked 30,000 yards of concrete pipes can be verified by this photograph. On the left of the main road to Canterbury the Rose Cabin tea rooms, the filling station and Howfield Manor, the home of local farmer Percy Mount, can just be seen.

William Lamberton working in the stained glass workshop of Samuel Caldwell jnr at 28 Blackfriars Street in the 1930s. Samuel Caldwell followed his father into the family's stained glass business and in due course became responsible for making and restoring the Cathedral's glass, a task he continued until into his eighties. After the last war the business was taken over by the Dean and Chapter of the Cathedral.

One of the city's chimney sweeps photographed at the Northgate Studio of R. Sinclair & Sons, c. 1900. Mr Sinclair moved into premises at 101 Northgate (near the junction with Union Street) at the turn of the century. At this time there were at least nine chimney sweeps in the city. The man shown in this 'cabinet' card is equipped with the tools of the trade.

William Page, an inspector (centre of front row), with his colleagues at the Canterbury post office in the early twentieth century. Back in 1866 the *Kentish Gazette* reported that 'the inhabitants of Canterbury will be glad to learn that it is the intention of the Post Office authorities to purchase the handsome and commodious residence on the King's Bridge, belonging to Mr Alfred Neame for the purpose of converting it into a Post Office'. The report went on to say 'There is a considerable breadth of ground to the back of the house which can be built upon and understand that the plans embrace the erection of spacious accommodation for the sorter's department . . . a separate entrance is proposed to be made from Lamb Lane [now Stour Street] to the rear of the front building for the mail carts, so that there will be no interruption to the street traffic.'

SCHOOLS & CHURCHES

A group of children at the Holy Cross and St Peter's School, 1931. The boys are (left to right): Freddie Butcher, Jasper Butcher, John Dyson, Michael Daniel and Mark Daniel. The girls are: Eva Hearn, Betty Woodcock, -?-. The school was opened in 1872 and in the 1920s could accommodate some 250 children; it closed in the 1970s and the site was subsequently developed for housing.

Girls at the old City Council school at St John's Place, Northgate, in the mid-1930s. The school was made up of three sections – girls, boys and infants. The girls in the left-hand group, back row (left to right) are: Peggy Kennett, Sylvia Ford, Nancy Tucker, Frances Racket; front row: Pat Garwood, Jean Gore and Joyce ?; middle group (standing): Brenda Sayer, Helen Long, Margaret Worthington. Right-hand group, back row: -?-, Pat Foster, Rose Williams, Rose Cogger, Joyce Edwards; front row: Pat Diddams, Ann Barton, Doreen Capper, Mary Carswell and Doris Fever.

Pupils at the City Council school with the trophies they had won at the Kent Music Festival just before the Second World War. The girls in the two back rows include Gladys Shepherd, Betsy O'Brien, Joan Gomm (head girl), Lilian Haines, Peggy Danton, Laura Thornby, Joan Edwards and Doreen Sutton. The three girls sitting are (left to right): Brenda Sayer, Sheila Muddle and Ruth Wilson and behind them Margaret Worthington, -?-, Pat Foster, Maisie Moys and Ann Barton.

Wincheap County Primary School's football team in the 1951/52 season with their trophies. The headmaster Cecil Bradshaw is on the far left and the master in charge of the team, Stanley Cousins on the far right. The boys shown are, back row (left to right): Brian Dobson, Walter Easey, Kenneth Honour, David James, Roy Thomas, David Gentle, David Jeffery, -?-; front row: Tony Blogg, Peter Cork, Brian Terry (captain), Roger Quested, David Mears.

The football team of the Wincheap County Primary School in the 1950/51 season with their teacher Stanley Cousins. Mr Cousins previously taught at the old St George's School and after seven years at Wincheap became headmaster of Hersden County Primary School in 1953. Mr Cousins remained there until he retired in 1977. When Wincheap School opened in 1940 it took pupils from three schools that closed, St Mildred's, St George's and St Mary Bredin.

Prefects at St Dunstan's (C. of E.) Modern School, 1956/57. Back row (left to right): -?-, David Mears, Chris Lane, Brian Rous, -?-, -?-, Peter Hart; front row: Michael O'Grady, David Jeffery, Keith Savage, Brian Howe, Barry Driscoll, David Gentle, -?-. St Dunstan's School closed in 1957 and was incorporated into the new Archbishop's School which opened in September of that year.

John Tyler retired as headmaster of the Frank Hooker School at the end of 1973 after nearly eighteen years in the post. He is seen here (on the extreme left) trying out one of his retirement gifts, an armchair, to the obvious delight of his wife Joan (on his right), Councillor Mrs K. Ellis and the deputy headmistress, Mrs B. Davies. Named after the chairman of the Education Committee, Frank Hooker, the secondary school opened in January 1956. In 1988 the name was changed to Canterbury High School.

Empire Day Parade at the Victoria Memorial Playing Fields, better known today as the Victoria Recreation Ground, 1920s. Girls from the Simon Langton School can be seen parading past the Mayor and Corporation. The ten acres of playing fields were developed at a cost of £1,600 and were opened in 1907. The wooden pavilion on the extreme left of this Frank Bailey photograph still survives.

Empire Day, 1928. The headmaster of St Dunstan's School (Mr J.B. Daniel) and boys salute the flag at the march past at the Victoria Recreation Ground. After a service at the Cathedral in the morning it was the custom for all the city's schools to parade later in the day. Taking the salute on this occasion was the mayor, William VanSittart Howard.

The St Edmund's School orchestra pictured at the school, *c.* 1947/48. The conductor is Donald Leggat and adult members of the orchestra include Dorothea Clayton (Leader) and staff members Philip Hollingworth and Mr and Mrs Maloney. One of the orchestra's soloists was schoolboy clarinettist Tony Coe (sitting to the left of the drums) who attended the Simon Langton Boys' School but received harmony lessons from Mr Leggat.

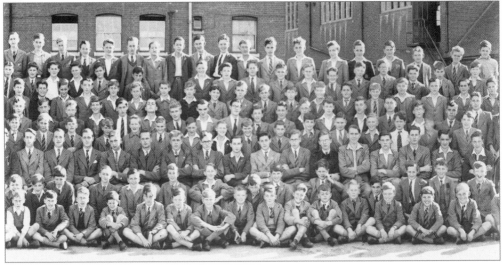

Simon Langton schoolboys (just part of the assembled school) in October 1946, my second year. Behind the group is the New Wing, built in 1913, which housed the gymnasium and staff common room. To the right is the block containing art and science rooms which ran parallel to Gravel Walk. These buildings survived the blitz unlike many others on the site. A number of prefects and sixth-formers as well as many members of my own year are seen.

The St Nicholas Church Choir, Thanington, photographed outside the church in 1928. In the centre of the middle row is the Revd Stanley Gordon Francis Wilson (Rector from 1925 to 1932) who was the city's Mayor in 1929 and 1930. Mr Wilson, who was a BLitt, AKCL, FRHistS, FSAScot, and JP, wrote a number of books including *With the Pilgrims to Canterbury*, published in 1934. In *A Short History of Thanington Church* he touches on the story that Thanington Churchyard was the spot associated with Gray's *Elegy*.

Dr Geoffrey Fisher, Archbishop of Canterbury, heading the procession to the new St Mary Bredin Church which he consecrated on 23 September 1957. Following the Archbishop are the Diocesan Registrar (Mr J.G. Pembrook), the Archdeacon of Canterbury (Ven. A Sargeant) and the Revd C. Waynforth (Rural Dean), Bishop Alfred Rose and the Bishop of Dover (Rt Revd L. Meredith), the Dean (Very Revd Hewlett Johnson) and local clergy. The procession is passing the Cross Keys public house at the junction of Old Dover Road and Oaten Hill.

Dr Henry Alford, Dean of Canterbury, in the late 1860s. During his time as Dean (1857–71) a number of reforms were implemented and sermons introduced into the Sunday evening services. He was also responsible for a number of famous hymns including, 'Come ye thankful people, come' and 'Ten thousand times ten thousand'. He gave his name to the Alford Poor Relief Association (later the Alford Aid Society) which worked on behalf of the poor and needy of the city until the 1970s.

The Cathedral Choir photographed by Fisk-Moore in 1928. In the centre of the middle row is the Organist and Choirmaster Dr C. Charlton Palmer, who served in that post from 1908 to 1936. On the right of the Precentor is Mr W.T. Harvey who was Assistant Organist for over forty years as well as being Musical Director for the Operatic Society, the Theatre Royal and later on the St George's Theatre. Among the Lay Clerks are Messrs Noakes, Coole, Baker, Johnson, Cresswell, Reid, Tophill and Noakes.

St Augustine's Cross was erected at Ebbsfleet, Thanet in 1884 to commemorate the landing of Augustine and his forty monks in AD 597. The cross was erected by Earl Granville, Lord Warden of the Cinque Ports and is based on the design of an ancient Saxon cross. The three lower panels on the cross depict St Alban, St Augustine and King Ethelbert. Augustine made his way to Canterbury where he was welcomed by the King and his Frankish wife, Bertha, already a Christian.

A postcard showing the suggested completion of the Benedictine Abbey of Saints Peter and Paul and Saint Augustine during Norman times. The abbey was founded by Augustine a few years after his arrival in the city in 597 and dedicated to Saints Peter and Paul. In 978 Archbishop Dunstan rededicated the enlarged abbey to include the name of St Augustine, who died in 605. He is commemorated by the church on 26 May of each year.

The Mothers' Union branch of St Nicholas Church, Thanington in 1946, the year the Canterbury Diocese celebrated the fiftieth anniversary of the organization. In the centre is the Revd Gilbert Finch, Rector from 1937 to 1946, and in front of him Mrs Finch. On either side of the banner are Mrs Mitchell (in the dark coat) and Mrs Reynard. The thirty-four-strong group also includes Mesdames Brice, Marsh (with her sister), Smithson-Birch, Willett, Sharp, Bailey, Newport, Winch, Vant, Curd, Gilbert, Carveth, Robbins, Goldfinch, Johnson and Page. The little girl in the front row is Sylvia Willett. Mr Finch went on to serve the parishes of Petham and Waltham before becoming Rector of Lydd in 1952. His last appointment was as Vicar of Elmsted with Hastingleigh in 1962.

Part of the procession celebrating the arrival of the Franciscan Friars in Canterbury 700 years earlier in September 1224. The procession, which is turning into Stour Street, is heading towards the Greyfriars where the assembled throng sang the 'Te Deum'. The photograph shows Cardinal Bourne heading a group which included some thirty nuns representing the Franciscan Missionaries of Mary and other Orders. The procession had begun at St Thomas's Church where the Cardinal had presided at a Pontifical High Mass.

The local Salvation Army Band, with bandmaster Fred Cox, August 1934. The Canterbury Temple Band was formed in 1889, eleven years after the first Salvation Army band came into existence and just three years after the Canterbury Temple Corps (no. 706) was founded. Through the years the band has played at many special services in the Cathedral, at open air meetings, in churches, schools, hospitals and old peoples' homes, etc.

The Martyrs' Memorial , *c.* 1899. This memorial was erected in 1899 and commemorates the forty-one Protestant martyrs burned to death between 1555 and 1558. The granite pillar was erected on the Martyrs' Field following a public appeal by the Mayor, Dean Farrar, Lord Northbourne and other local dignitaries. The martyrs, many of whom had been incarcerated in Canterbury Castle, comprised ten women and thirty-one men, including John Bland, Vicar of Adisham and John Frankesh, Vicar of Rolvenden. A poster giving details of the adjoining land to be developed as the Martyrs' Field Road Estate is also seen.

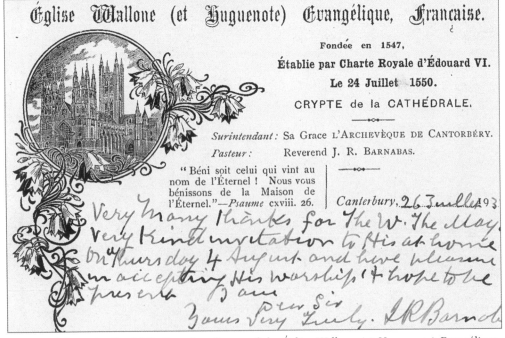

A postcard from the Revd J.R. Barnabas, Pastor of the Église Wallone (et Huguenote) Evangélique, Française, written to the Town Clerk in 1932. The Protestant refugees from the Walloon districts of Belgium and their neighbours from France were given permission to worship in the west crypt of the Cathedral during the latter part of the sixteenth century. The current members of the church (now known as the Église Protestante Française de Cantorbéry) now worship in the adjoining Black Prince's Chantry.

Celebrations commemorating Queen Victoria's Diamond Jubilee in 1897. Some 4,000 children of the city's Sunday Schools, with about 400 of their teachers, marched from the Cathedral to the St Lawrence Cricket ground. They were accompanied by the Cavalry Band, the City Band and the local Boys' Brigade Band. Some of the children are seen here in St Lawrence Road with the old Bat and Ball Inn on the left. The banner which can be seen is that of the Ragged School contingent who numbered seventy-five.

The interior of the old Congregational Church (Countess of Huntingdon's Connection) situated in Watling Street, c. 1900. This photograph was taken from the gallery, looking towards the large organ behind the raised dais. Built in 1863 at a cost of £2,100, the church was damaged beyond repair in an air raid which followed the main blitz on the city. Eliza and Elizabeth Lefevre, daughters of William, were both in the choir at this church which they attended for some seventy years.

Canon Gerald Thompson, Vicar of St Gregory's Church from 1918 to 1939, with children of the parish in the late 1930s. At a meeting of the Public Assistance Committee in 1939, Councillor J.G.B. Stone paid tribute to Mr Thompson, who had previously served on the old Board of Guardians, referring to the fact that the vicar had represented the largest and perhaps poorest parish of the city and that 'if any parish priest had ever worn himself out in the strenuous and untiring devotion to the call of his cure, that might very truly be said of the late Canon'.

St Gregory's Church Choir outside the old church now used by Christ Church College, early 1950s. Along with the Vicar, the Revd Donald Pharoah, and the Curate, the Revd George Aylen, the men include Percy Prebble, John Coupland, Basil Johnson, Harold Hart, Leslie Collins (holding the cross), Fred Duckett, John Page, Bob Sarbutt and Cyril Hadfield. The young men and boys include Robin Fenn, John Fryer, Haydon Davis, Ashley Fryer, Ian Hadfield, John Gammon, Louis Kennett, Roy Baker, Bruce Wilkinson, Douglas Goddard, Nicky Swain and Kenny Burrows.

SPORT, LEISURE & LOCAL DANCE BANDS

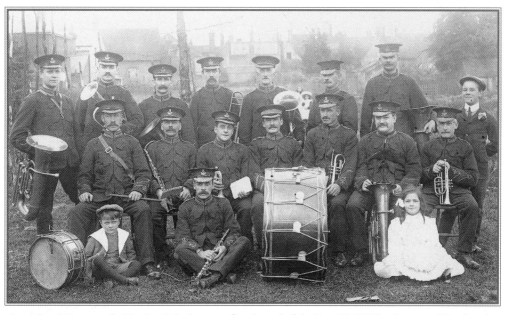

A city band photographed by Frank Bailey just after the end of the First World War. It may well be that this is an early picture of the Canterbury Silver Band (later renamed the Canterbury City Prize Band) which was very active throughout the 1920s and 1930s.

The monument to the famous Kent and England cricketer Fuller Pilch, which was erected in St Gregory's churchyard soon after his death in 1870. Born in Norfolk, he first settled at Malling and played for Kent from 1836 to 1854. He moved to the city in 1842 and became the first groundsman at the St Lawrence Cricket Ground in 1847. It is said that he was the greatest batsman before W.G. Grace. In October 1978 the monument, without the obelisk, was removed to the St Lawrence Ground. The plaque showing Pilch at the wicket – copied from G.F. Watt's famous lithograph – has now been removed.

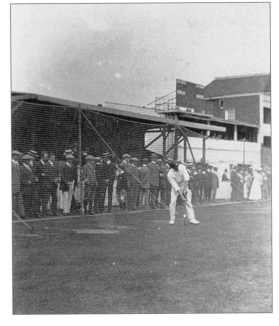

George Hirst, the Yorkshire and England cricketer, pictured in the nets at the St Lawrence Ground, 1911. The white shed and telegraph office adjoining the pavilion were built in 1892. The ground floor was used for storage of nets, etc. with an upper section for the scorers and press. This building and the wooden stand were demolished to make way for the concrete stand which opened in 1926.

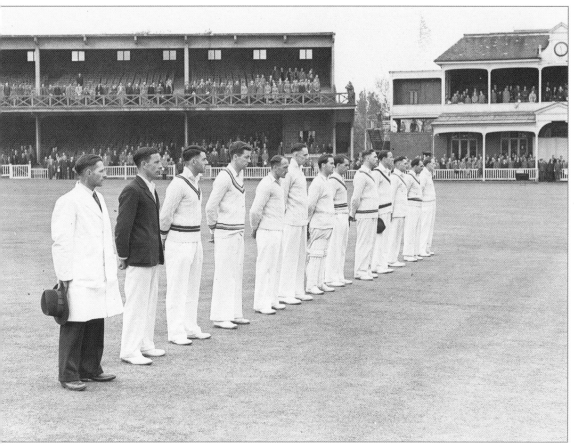

The Kent cricket team at the St Lawrence Ground, 18 May 1946, when they played Yorkshire in their first home game after the war. Both teams lined up to pay their respects to players who were killed in the hostilities including two former Kent captains, G.B. Legge and F.G.H. Chalk, as well as the famous Yorkshire and England slow bowler Hedley Verity. The players shown, left to right after the umpire, are: Claude Lewis (12th man), Peter Sunnucks, Doug Wright, Tom Spencer, Norman Harding, Godfrey Evans, David Clark, Jack Martin, Tom Pearce, Leslie Todd, Leslie Ames, Bryan Valentine (captain). This was the first match I ever attended at the ground and to my dismay Kent were beaten by an innings and 91 runs. A serious blow was to befall the side in the following year when Norman Harding died in September 1947, just a few weeks after playing against the South Africans. The pavilion, with its famous clock, was built in 1900 and the concrete stand in 1926.

Members of the Beverley Cricket Club photographed at the St Lawrence Ground in the early 1950s. Those standing are (left to right): R. Greenway, R. Forwood, F. Stotesbury, E. Holness, W. Stace, D. Smith, H. West, B. Rogers, C. Swain, -?-, F. Longley, -?-; front row: M. Kingsford, V. Luxton, E. Miles, W. Goodwin, W. Parker (President), N. West, C. Rogers, H. Mayes, R. Jordan. The Beverley Club was founded in 1835 and in 1870 the original club joined with the Kent County team to form the Kent County Cricket Club. In the 1950s the club ran three Saturday teams and two Thursday XIs, and members of the latter are seen here.

The Canterbury Co-op cricket team in the early 1950s. The team played on Thursday afternoons when the city's shops closed early and most of the fixtures were against other shop XIs, e.g. Lefevres and other local Co-op sides. Back row (left to right): ? Anslow (scorer), J. Stockbridge, H. West, J. Adams, L. Silk, H. West snr (umpire); middle row: N. West, R. Gilpin, T. Ticehurst, J. Goddard, W. Goodwin; front row: A. Brown and G. Percival. The photograph was taken on the Chislet Colliery Welfare Ground at Hersden.

The Post Office cricket team and officials photographed at Wincheap Grove in 1909 with their trophy for winning the Canterbury League Cup. During that season only four teams contested the league – Post Office, Finn & Sons, the Gas Works and Press Amalgamated. St Andrew's Presbyterian Church can just be seen in the distance. Over the years Wincheap Grove hosted a variety of sports but was best known as the home of the Canterbury Waverley Football Club in the 1920s and 1930s.

The Canterbury City football team in the season 1955/56, when they were managed by Bill Higgins (ex-Everton and Bogotá), his second year with the club. The players are back row (left to right): George Pope, Bob Morley, 'Pip' Skinner, Tommy Francis, Bob Hawkins, John McIvor; front row: Norman Hooper, Roy Evans, Bill Higgins, Tommy Tippett, Les Stevens. In this season the team reached three semi-finals and were losing finalists in the Kent Senior Shield.

The Bat and Trap team from the Woodman's Arms public house, Wincheap, 1933. The team were photographed before they set out for Brighton on an outing. Back row (left to right): S. May, Percy Martin, Jack Sackett, Fred Chapman, 'Happy' Attwood, Bert Sackett, Jimmy Gower, Charlie Tomsett, Percy Sackett, Norman Rye, Bob Cramp jnr, Alf Bundock, -?-; front row: Teddy Long, Percy Chapman, Tom Sackett, -?-, Bob Cramp snr. The names of the two boys are not known.

Members of the Bat and Trap team at 'Ye Olde Beverlie Inn' in the early 1930s. The game of bat and trap originated in the area and it is said it was first played at the 'Beverlie'. Until some forty years ago the licensee of this sixteenth-century inn also carried out the duties of parish clerk. Walter Browning (third from the left in the middle row) was a member of the team which was probably just about to set off on an outing.

Indian club swinging was a popular pastime about a hundred years ago and this H.B. Collis photograph shows a group of local boys with their clubs. One description of an Indian club says that it is usually a wooden club, shaped like a tenpin, that is swung for exercise. It is difficult to think how some of these angelic-looking boys got on with their fairly long clubs. In his fascinating book *An East Kent Family* (published in 1956) Frank Twyman tells how he was the leader of a squad which swung Indian clubs when he was at Simon Langton Boys' School, and he goes into some detail about the technicalities of grip, etc. He might well be in this photograph as he was talking about the year 1891, about the same time as this photograph was taken. The photographer, Henry B. Collins, started his business at 47a St George's Street in 1889 and moved to his Westgate Studio at 33 St Peter's Street in 1894. He continued until the First World War when the studio was taken over by Ackland and Youngman.

The Canterbury Hockey Club 'Thursday' team photographed at their ground in Nackington Road during the 1922 season. Those shown in the back row include Messrs F. Phillips, Eric Bradley, C.E. Wake, Songhurst and Stanley Jennings. Among those in the front row are Messrs F. Cornfoot, Couldray, J.B. Thompson and C. Colling-Baugh. The club played on a number of different grounds after the last war but now have a permanent home at the old Polo Farm Ground in Littlebourne Road.

Members of a local tennis club who played on courts in Sturry Road in the late 1920s. Among the ladies in the group are Winnie Bradley, Olive Goodban, Margaret Henderson, Dorothy Read and members of the Oliver, Watson and Bourne families. The men include Gerry Gascoigne, Bert Amos, Hubert Jarvis, George Henderson, Harold Goodban, Charles Read, Sidney Todd, Leslie Read and Reg Pettyfer.

Canterbury Cine Club members rehearsing a scene from their 1937 production entitled *The Way of the Amateur*. The club had accommodation at the old Prince of Wales Institute in Northgate where sets were built and indoor scenes filmed. This particular film told the story of a rather fanciful thespian who actually played the rear end of a donkey but is of interest because it was filmed in colour, which had to be specially ordered from Kodak. The large lights were made by Bill Entwistle at his workshop at Grove Court, Upstreet and were lined by thousands of pieces of silver paper salvaged from cigarette packets. Members shown in the back row (left to right) are: C. Sparke, -?-, E. Cardew (behind the camera), Rob Williams (the focus-puller), Dr A Brett, S. Pentin and Jack Blundell; front row: Anita Goulden (continuity girl), Rita Blundell, John Mann (director), -?-, and W. Lillywhite (with back to camera). In 1934 the *Kent Herald* reported that the club was in need of more ladies to come forward to take part in their productions.

The Old Stagers photographed during their jubilee in 1892. They came into being as the result of the Hon. Frederick Ponsonby, who played against Kent in 1841, being asked to bring an England XI to Canterbury in 1842 and also to perform in the evening at the old theatre in Orange Street. The Old Stagers set up their headquarters at the Royal Fountain Hotel and when the Theatre Royal was built by T.S.Cooper in 1861 played there for many years. Sidney Cooper's son Nevill was a keen member and can be seen in the photograph third from the right in the back row.

The Canterbury Operatic Society photographed for their production of *The Gondoliers*, 1963. Edred Wright, the Society's Musical Director, can be seen in the second row (fourth from the left) with Marguerite Astle, the Producer, on his left. Founded in 1906, the Society's production in 1963 was their thirty-third. Some of the members in the photograph are still active in the Society today, including Maurice Spillett, the current President.

Bob Simmons, leader of the popular Blue Shadows Dance Band which he formed in the early 1950s. Mr Simmons began his musical career when he took violin lessons with Alex Reid at the age of eight. Later on he took up the saxophone and at the age of fifteen was playing with local dance bands, including that of Eddie Newport. For many years the band played at the popular dances held at the Drill Hall before transferring to the Abbot's Barton Hotel and finally to Slatter's Hotel.

Bob Simmons and his Blue Shadows Dance Band in the 1960s. Left to right: Alf Stroud (piano), Ted Weatherall (saxophone), Len Housego (bass), Bob Simmons (saxophone) and Stan Clozier (drums). This photograph was taken at the Nunnery Fields Hospital at one of the staff functions. Len Housego was the regular bass player in the band throughout its near twenty-year existence.

The Blue Shadows Dance Band at Slatter's Hotel in the 1960s. The members of the band are (left to right): Len Housego (bass), Peter Pinder (drums), Veronica Price (vocalist), David Barnett (piano) and Bob Simmons, leader (saxophone). The band played for the regular Saturday night 'Dine and Dance' events at the hotel for a good number of years until it disbanded in the autumn of 1970. (Reproduced with permission of Kent Messenger Group Newspapers).

Bob Simmons and his band playing at the Winter Gardens Theatre, Margate in the 1960s. In this eight-piece orchestra were (left to right): Alf Stroud (piano), George Coe (alto saxophone), Len Housego (bass), Bob Simmons (alto saxophone), -?- (saxophone), Stan Clozier (drums), Ted Weatherall (saxophone) and Tommy Glasgow (trumpet).

Members of the Eddie Newport Dance Band, *c.* 1953. Left to right: Hugh 'Slim' Mitchell, Sid Downs, Marshall Crayford, Eddie Newport, Tony Coe and George Coe. Eddie Newport was a popular local musician who led a number of bands from 1920, including the Cantuar Dance Band and the Regal Band, the latter so called because it performed at the Regal (Cinema) Ballroom until it was blitzed in 1942. The band then transferred to the Foresters' Hall in the High Street for a number of years.

Eddie Newport and his orchetra on stage at the Dreamland Ballroom, Margate in the mid-1950s. They had an enthusiastic following at this ballroom, the venue at which they bowed out in 1956. Eddie can be seen at the piano with Stan Whitworth (bass), Hugh Mitchell (drums), Marshall Crayford and Les Parsons (trumpets). Sitting are the saxophonists George Coe, Freddie Morris and Jack Buckland.

An advertising postcard for Norman Steele and his County Dance Band who were local favourites in the 1930s. In 1931 they finished fourth in a county-wide dance band competition organized by the *Kent Messenger*. The other members featured on the card are (left to right): Jimmy Head, Harold Price, George Coe and Jack Wheatley. The Hales Place Pavilion was one venue where they played – tickets were 2*s*. plus an extra 1*s*. 6*d*. for breakfast after the dance finished at 1 a.m.

The County Dance Band on board a carnival float photographed at Thanington in the 1930s. Those seen are (left to right): Norman Steele (leader and pianist), George Coe (saxophone), Jimmy Head (saxophone), Len Cheal (drums) and Jack Wheatley (banjo). Arthur Parker, the band's trumpeter, was apparently late for the photograph. The dance advertised was to be at the County Hall which was situated above Martin's store in St George's Street.

Tony Coe, who followed in his father's footsteps as a clarinettist and saxophonist. Tony had clarinet lessons in Canterbury with Paddy Purcell and played with a number of local bands, sometimes alongside his father. After Army service in the Buffs he settled for the life of a jazz musician and played with Joe Daniels, Nat Gonella and Al Fairweather before his first spell with the Humphrey Lyttleton band. He was also offered a place in the famous Count Basie band, but did not take up this invitation. Tony is noted for playing on the soundtrack of the *Pink Panther* film and for composing a number of orchestral pieces and a film score.

Clarinettists George Coe (on left) and Tony Coe (centre) with band leader Ken Grieff at the Talisman Ballroom in St Peter's Street (now the August Moon Chinese restaurant). Both George and Tony played for Ken's band at this popular venue in the 1950s. I was a classmate of Tony's at the Simon Langton School so have been very interested in his career, which has seen him receive an honorary Doctor of Music degree from the University of Kent in 1988 and the prestigious Jazz Par award in 1994; the first non-American musician to receive this.

Frederic Hargraves and his orchestra, with vocalists Daphne John and Trevor Paige in the 1960s. This dance orchestra was very popular after the Second World War, Frederic Hargraves and his Swingtette having been the resident band at the Odeon Ballroom in St Peter's Street from about 1942 to the late 1940s. The band provided 'music in the modern manner' and in the war years charged entrance fees ranging from 1s. to 2s. depending on the night of the week.

Billy Elliott and his dance band c. 1946/7. The members of the band, who played at venues all round the local area are (left to right): Doug Rigden (bass), Jimmy Head (tenor saxophone), Hugh Mitchell (drums), George Coe (alto saxophone) and Billy Elliott (piano). A number of the members had previously played for the County Dance Band before the last war.

STREETS & BUILDINGS

St Stephen's Hill, looking towards the city, c. 1900. The wooded area on the left has now been fully developed with Downs Road going off to the left at the bottom of the hill. The photograph shows how rural this area of St Stephen's was nearly a hundred years ago.

Lady Wootton's Green looking towards Broad Street and the Cathedral in the 1880s. The green was an attractive area surrounded by trees; thankfully this open space still survives today, although the roads on either side are usually filled with traffic. The green was named after Lady Wootton, who, with her husband, lived for a while in a royal palace which Henry VIII created among the ruins of St Augustine's Abbey.

Part of St Radigund's Street and Abbot's Mill, *c.* 1880. The mill derived its name from the time when an earlier mill was in the ownership of St Augustine's Abbey, although it was known as Denne's Mill after being purchased by Thomas Denne from local artist Sidney Cooper in the 1890s.

Part of Old Dover Road at its junction with Nunnery Fields and Oaten Hill as it looked before the First World War. On the extreme left is no. 77, the property of Frederick Muir (carpenter, joiner and undertaker) and further down is the greengrocer's shop of J.C. Pine. The five three-storey houses were built in the early 1890s and replaced a line of tumbledown cottages known as 'Rats Row'. Opposite the cottages was an old oast house adjoining the Cross Keys public house.

Hanover Lodge in Hanover Place (renamed Roper Road in 1918), the home of Robert Stockdale, 1915. The property, no. 50, was later called Holme Lodge and is now known as Chaucer House. In 1918 some eighty residents from Hanover Road and Hanover Place petitioned the council to have 'the name of their roads changed', pointing out that they considered it a 'distasteful association with the name . . .'.

The East Kent Model Engineering Co. shop, 21b Burgate Street before the Second World War. It was situated adjacent to the premises of W. Stephenson & Son (on the right of the picture) who were ladies' and gentlemens' tailors. Both these properties were destroyed in the bombing raids of June 1942 when large sections of Burgate Street were blitzed.

Shops on the south side of Burgate Street, *c.* 1910. On the extreme right were nos 52, housing the Co-operative Society Ltd., 53, Philpot's Bookshop (old books, prints and stamps) and 54, George Dukes (watchmaker and jeweller). The printing works of J. Hayes was at no. 55 and J. Moys' general shop was at no. 56 on the corner of Iron Bar Lane. Beyond the lane can be seen the Crown Inn. All of these properties were destroyed in the 1942 blitz.

The north side of Burgate Street in the late 1930s. On the left are Carver & Staniforth (booksellers) at no. 20, Irvine Williams (furrier) at nos 18/19, C.H. Smith (tailor) at no. 17, and Lenleys (soft furnishers) at no. 16. All these properties were destroyed in an air raid on 11 October 1940 which left nine people dead. The victims included Miss Gertrude Carver, a partner in the bookshop, and Mr Williams together with his assistants and customers.

The tower of St Mary Magdalen Church in Burgate Street in the early twentieth century. Next to the tower can be seen the hardware shop of F. Bligh with a fine array of tin baths on display and the weatherboarded Crown Inn on the corner of Iron Bar Lane. Both the shop and the inn were destroyed in the Second World War. The church tower, dating from 1503, now contains the baroque monument to the Whitfield family (c. 1680) previously housed in the church. The remainder of the church had been pulled down in 1871.

Shops at 36–38 High Street in the 1920s. Madame Stuart (milliner) was at no. 36, Arthur Bozon (confectioner) at no. 37 and Aitchison & Co. Ltd. (opticians) at no. 38. Walter Cozens, a builder and local historian, had his shop at no. 37 in the 1890s and describes the building, especially the cellar, in his book *Old Canterbury* published in 1906. It is interesting to note that no. 36 now has a gable matching that of no. 37.

The front of the Refectory of Blackfriars Monastery, photographed by J.G. Charlton in the early twentieth century. At that time the Unitarians used the building, although there were tenements on the ground floor and the women and children on the steps were probably some of the families who lived there. The Blackfriars, or Dominicans, commenced building in 1236; the refectory and the guest hall are the only buildings that have survived.

Terraced houses on the northern side of St George's Place in the early twentieth century. With their attractive louvred window shutters, these town houses were especially popular with the professional classes of the time. Most of the properties on the northern side from no. 5 along to the junction with Lower Chantry Lane were destroyed by fire in the 1942 blitz.

The imposing house called Pinecroft was situated in Barton Fields (originally numbered 21 New Dover Road), 1920s. For many years it was the home of Cecil Kingsford, the local solicitor, but in the 1920s it became St Helen's School for Girls under its principal Miss Winifred German. The property became a private dwelling again during the 1930s.

A section of Broad Street during the First World War. The area behind the iron railings and the cottages numbered 104 to 109 were cleared away for road widening and development of the city's first municipal car park in 1931. The properties on the right leading down to Lady Wootton's Green were all destroyed by enemy action in the last war. This scene is of interest as it shows how narrow Broad Street was before 1931.

Part of St Stephen's Road looking towards the Manwood Almshouses in the 1920s. The large house is the old Rectory (now called Glebe House) which faces towards St Stephen's Green and the church. The house is now the St Stephen's Surgery. Part of the brick wall on the left hand side still survives too.

Glebe House (rear view) in St Stephen's Road, which for many years was used as the Rectory for the parish of St Stephen (Hackington), in the 1930s. Built in the early eighteenth century, the house is a grade II listed property and reverted to its original name when a new Rectory was built in the garden during 1961. St Stephen's Church can just be seen to the left of the house.

St Stephen's Green in the 1930s. The building on the left is Glebe Cottage near the entrance to Beverley Dairy Farm. The cottage, dating from the sixteenth century, is situated near to Glebe House in St Stephen's Road. This postcard, sent in 1936, was written by John Howard who lived in the property at the time.

Roper House in St Dunstan's Street, before the First World War. Originally the home of Frederick Flint, owner of the adjacent brewery, it had become a Ladies School by 1912 and subsequently the home of Dr Harold Wacher. In 1939 it was known as Roper House Hotel and in the late 1940s became the headquarters of the Royal School of Church Music. In 1955 it was taken over by the National Institute for the Deaf.

This attractive house stood at the bottom of Artillery Street near its junction with Victoria Row and was photographed by Edward Coomber in July 1968. The White House was quite out of character with the adjacent houses but suffered the same fate as the remaining properties in Artillery Street. They were all demolished a year or so later to make way for a total redevelopment of the area.

Cotton Mill Row Cottages were situated in Broad Oak Road not far from the junction of St Stephen's Road and Kingsmead Road. They were originally built for workers at the cotton mill located on the back stream of the River Stour by James Callaway in 1791. Hasted described it as 'on the river at Shoal-oak'. The cottages were served by a communal water pump situated in the bank opposite; they were demolished in the late 1950s before the road was widened a few years later.

The rear of Cotton Mill Row backing on to a branch of the River Stour (the houses facing the row are in Stour View) in the 1950s. It is said that the mill employed fifty women and children but after Mr Callaway's death in 1807 it ceased working and was pulled down. At one time James Callaway was Master of the Silk Weavers and invented the famous 'Canterbury Muslins'.

Part of Ivy Lane in the 1920s. The photograph shows the cottages numbered 40a and 41 and then 42–46. The latter group formed a fourteenth-century Wealden House which was restored in the 1960s to become one dwelling called The Hall. Ivy Lane, in former times known as Lodderelane (Beggars' Lane), has a fascinating history which has been recorded in a booklet entitled *Ivy Lane Remembered*, published in 1994 by the Local History Group of the Oaten Hill and District Society.

A view of Church Hill, Harbledown showing the Coach and Horses public house and the adjoining shop, in the 1890s. The Coach and Horses belonged to Flint & Sons Ltd. of St Dunstan's Brewery, founded in 1797. Further down the hill on the left hand side is the entrance to the hospital of St Nicholas, founded in 1084 by Archbishop Lanfranc for the relief of lepers.

The entrance to Canterbury Cemetery in Westgate Court Avenue in the early twentieth century. The architect, John Green Hall, designed the building which has a central spire with two flanking chapels. The cemetery, comprising 12 acres, was opened on 4 July 1877 at a cost of £9,000; an additional 8 acres were purchased in 1923. Mr Hall was also responsible for the design of St Thomas's Roman Catholic Church and St Andrew's Presbyterian Church.

The High Street on a peaceful Sunday morning, 1910. The policeman on duty at the junction with Mercery Lane and St Margaret's Street was PC Walter Maple. It is hard to imagine that he was controlling the traffic but the lady with the parasol and the gentleman in the frock coat are safely crossing the street, probably *en route* to the cathedral. The Capital and Counties Bank Ltd. (now Lloyds) can be seen on the left and on the right Hilton's shop sign is prominent.

The Prince and Princess of Wales visited the city on 29 May 1897 primarily to open the newly restored Chapter House in the Cathedral. It was, however, an opportunity for the citizens to celebrate 'the presence among us of the popular Heir Apparent to the British throne and Empire'. The photograph shows the entrance to the West station, where the Royal party arrived at 12.20 p.m. with a triumphal arch of evergreens bidding the visitors 'Welcome'. On the reverse was the message 'Au Revoir' for their return to the station.

'God Bless the Prince and Princess of Wales' was the wording on the banner put up for the Royal visit at the Buttermarket end of Mercery Lane. A contemporary newspaper report said that 'festoons of evergreen formed a Bower, suspended from which were some baskets of the choicest flowers and a large number of Japanese lanterns'. Two venetian poles held the banner in place and looking down the lane 'the sight was a most enchanting one'.

St George's Gate also boasted a triumphal arch carrying the message 'Long Live the Prince'. The approach was decorated with a series of 'lattice work arcades covered with evergreens and with their pedestals most cleverly and effectively adorned with growing plants in full colour'. Mr Edwin Ellis of the St Lawrence Steam Laundry was responsible for the arch; he had originally intended to build a reproduction of Tower Bridge but there wasn't sufficient space.

A section of the River Stour looking towards the High Street with the old Weavers' House on the right, and what is commonly called the Alchemist's Tower on the left, in the 1890s. This scene predates the restoration of The Weavers and shows only three gables on the house. The origin of the tower is a mystery, though it was probably built towards the end of the eighteenth century and may have formed part of the cemetery buildings of nearby All Saints' Church.

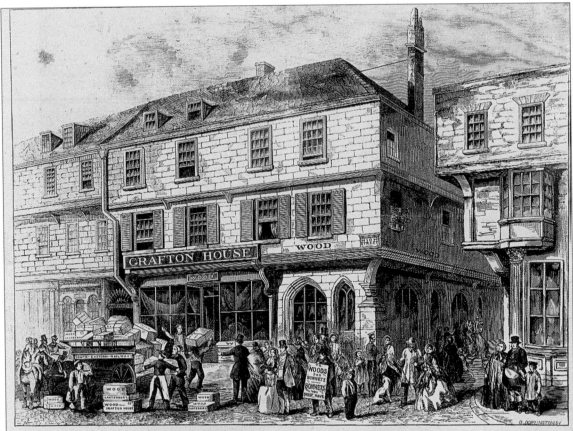

The Chekers of the Hope,

Which every man doth know.---CHAUCER.

Was Built A.D., 1100.

GEORGE WOOD'S BABY LINEN, HOSIERY, GLOVE and STAY WAREHOUSE, is an extensive building, at the corner of Mercery Lane, in the High Street, Canterbury (as the above engraving shows), known by the name of "Chaucer's Inn;" it is now converted into shops, but was formerly an Inn; the same mentioned by Chaucer as being the one to which the pilgrims came from the "Talbot," in Southwark, London, to visit the shrine of St. Thomas-a-Becket. It is a good specimen of the architecture of the time, and though now nearly 800 years old, will withstand many a wintry blast. It appears to have been built in the form of a quadrangle, having an open court-yard in the middle, The stories, or suites of rooms, projected in front over one another, and were supported by pillars, forming a colonade, which has been removed; but the corner shop, indeed, shows by arches each way, in what manner the ground-floor was built.

An engraving showing the Chequers of the Hope Inn on the corner of the High Street and Mercery Lane in the mid-1850s. It was built at the end of the fourteenth century to provide accommodation for the growing number of pilgrims to the city and boasted a large courtyard surrounded by internal galleries. Much of this was destroyed by fire in 1865. For many years the property (no. 1 and Grafton House, no. 2) was used by George Wood as his 'Baby Linen, Hosiery, Glove and Stay Warehouse', but it is possible that the business did not continue after the fire. The building on the opposite corner of Mercery Lane dates back to the sixteenth century and since 1930 has housed Boots the Chemists.

The interior of the Masonic Temple, St Peter's Street. The temple was designed by John Green Hall, the City Surveyor, and the foundation stone was laid on 4 March 1880. It was consecrated to the gathering of the 'free and accepted brethren' and a number of Lodges and Chapters have met here over the past 117 years.

The Castle Hotel at 30 Castle Street, at the junction with Wincheap Green in the late 1920s. Edward Leavers was the licensee at this time and among those standing outside is 'Drummer Jack', one of the most colourful characters around the city. His real name was Johnnie Spriggs and as a young man he served as a drummer in the 3rd Battalion of the Buffs. Wincheap Green was one area where he entertained locals and visitors alike. The Castle Hotel was demolished in 1963 to make way for the Wincheap roundabout.

An aerial view showing the St George's area before the development of the old Whitefriars site, January 1962. Some of the buildings and the old St Mary Bredin churchyard can be seen in Gravel Walk and Riceman's store is under construction in St George's Lane. The old wall on the site of the Langton Boys' School can be seen in splendid isolation. The car parks at the Marlowe Theatre and along the city wall in the old cattle market seem to be full.

St George's Street showing David Greig's shop on the corner of Canterbury Lane in the late 1950s. The shop was built in 1953 to a unique design by Robert Paine & Partners, who were awarded a RIBA Bronze Medal in 1956. David Greig closed the business in the late 1970s and the panel showing the emblem of a thistle was removed before Woolworth & Co. took over the premises. More recently the property has been registered as a Grade II listed building.

Tonford Manor at Thanington in the 1890s. The Manor of Tonford belonged to John de Toniford in the reign of Henry III and some years later the house was rebuilt to include round guard towers and a surrounding moat. Situated close to the River Stour, the location was a favourite spot of the local painter Sidney Cooper and the house features in a painting completed in 1892. Christopher Hassall, the dramatist, lived here in the late 1950s and early 1960s. An interesting novel by Sardius Hancock called *Tonford Manor*, set in pre-Reformation times, was published in 1903.

A group of soldiers marching along Rhodaus Town towards the station in the 1890s. With their pillbox hats they might well have been members of the Royal East Kent Mounted Rifles and were obviously popular with the young boys looking on. On the bank to the right can be seen the old St Mary Bredin School erected in 1860 and now used by the Canterbury Motor Co. The large building in the centre was the Canterbury Olympia Skating Rink later called the Pavilion.

A peaceful scene at St George's Gate, looking towards St George's Street in the 1890s. The cattle market is behind the iron railings on the left and beyond the entrance to St George's Terrace (on the left) is the East Kent Club. The properties on the right include the St George's Supply Stores (no. 2), the tailor's shop of E. Williams & Son (no. 3) and the photographic studio of James Craik (no. 4) on the corner of Burgate Lane. The loss of these buildings in the Second World War has completely altered the appearance of this part of the city.

The giant treadwheel (or treadmill) installed in the upper storey of the Bell Harry Tower in the Cathedral towards the end of the fifteenth century. John Wastell was the architect responsible for building the tower and used the wheel for hauling up the thousands of bricks and stone required. The wheel, which is situated above the fan-vaulted lantern of the tower, would have been worked with just two or three men; it is still used from time to time.

The Congregational Church in Guildhall Street with its imposing front entrance, *c.* 1900. The church was built in 1876, replacing an earlier chapel, and closed in 1948 after being declared unsafe for use. The building was purchased by William Lefevre Ltd. (Debenhams) and incorporated into their premises. The church was designed by John Green Hall who was responsible for other local churches.

The ruins of the seventh-century church of St Pancras in the grounds of St Augustine's Abbey in the 1890s. Situated to the east of the main abbey, it was at one time thought to have been King Ethelbert's idol-house before his conversion. Major excavation work on the site commenced in about 1900.

Canterbury's South Station, looking towards South Canterbury Road in the 1930s. The Elham Valley line between Folkestone (Cheriton) and Canterbury was opened in 1889 after five years' work. The white station building was fairly modest and was at its busiest in Cricket Week. Houses were later to be built at the start of Ethelbert Road on the right and all the land in the foreground is now taken up by the Kent and Canterbury Hospital. The line was converted to a single track in 1931 and finally closed in 1947.

Part of Lower Bridge Street looking towards the premises of Invicta Motors Ltd. in the late 1960s. Next to them is the Brickies' butcher's shop and the new offices of the Royal Insurance Co. Ltd. The 'closing down' sale notice in Twyman's shop window on the right gives a clue to the fact that their premises and the adjoining Modern Floral Services shop were about to be demolished to make way for the St George's roundabout and the continuation of the ring road.

THE SECOND WORLD WAR

St George's Street, with severely damaged St George's Church, a day or two after the Baedeker raid of 1 June 1942. The extent of the damage on the south side of the street can be gauged from this scene, which also records one of the barrage balloons flying over the city – this can just be seen to the left of the tall building.

The remains of the Society of Friends' Meeting House at 10 Canterbury Lane (on the left) after the devastation of the 1 June blitz in 1942. The photograph, looking towards Burgate, shows firemen still damping down the fires in buildings on the right of the lane. The Meeting House opened in March 1688, some years after George Fox had made a number of visits to the city, and was extensively altered in 1772. It had built-in seats on four sides with an open space in the middle which could accommodate 100 members. At the time of the blitz it was the oldest non-conformist place of worship in the city.

A group of the Royal Observer Corps who maintained an unbroken watch at Cockering Farm, Thanington from 24 August 1939 to 12 May 1945. Although their main duties were intelligence work for the RAF Fighter Command and the monitoring of aircraft in distress, they gave information which caused air raid warnings to be sounded. This photograph dates from 1945 and shows the members of Post B2 (in Group 1) outside their bunker at the farm. Back row (left to right): J. Elvidge, A. Smith, S. Conrath, W. Kennett, H. Layzell, W. Yates, E. Palmer, R. Brown, R. Maylam, D. Andrews, H. Nicholson, R. Page, G. Christian, J. Patterson; front row: H. Crawford, R. Finnis, J. Roberts, H. Ashenden, S. Wake (Chief Observer), R. Wright (Leading Observer), H. Reed, Mrs K. Miles, S. Jennings.

An ARP First Aid Party pictured at their headquarters at Orchard House, Wincheap, in the early days of the Second World War. Harry Lye, the Station Officer (with back to camera) is seen briefing other members. Left to right: Tom Sayer, Harry Lye, Bob Hadlow, -?-, 'Buddy' O'Neil and Arthur Goodwin. The private (Vauxhall) car used by the party was modified to carry stretchers, etc.

Members of the Civil Defence Corps in the early days of the Second World War by their post at the Poor Priests' Hospital in Stour Street. Left to right: Reg Mitchell, Charlie Sefton, David Featherstone and George Coe. Canterbury's plans for National Service were well underway by early 1939 and various branches of Air Raid Precautions, e.g. wardens, rescue and first aid teams and ambulance drivers, were formed in readiness for the inevitable conflict that was to follow.

HRH The Duke of Kent inspecting members of the Civil Defence Services when he visited the city, 3 May 1941. The group nearest the camera were members of an ambulance unit, the 'ambulance' being a converted East Kent 'bus which was adapted as a mobile dressing station. Those identified in the rear rank are (left to right): Mrs Reynolds, Helen Pring, Mr Holness; front row (left to right): 'Blossom' Maple, -?-, Mabel Scott, Nellie Wilson, May Birt.

The junior section of the Civil Defence Corps pictured outside the Cathedral. The occasion was probably the Thanksgiving Service and Victory March held on 13 May 1945. The photograph shows a number of ladies in the line-up and two Royal Enfield motor cycles, reg. nos BJG 374 and 375. Among those identified are Don Worthington, Peter Prebble, Ernie Lovering and Bert West. They acted as messengers between the various ARP posts in the city.

Part of St George's Terrace after the bombing in June 1942. From the Sun Building, which stood on the corner of St George's Street. the terrace ran upwards from no. 1 and the properties shown are probably nos 1 to 5. It would appear from the ladders in place that workmen were about to begin the demolition of the damaged buildings.

A post-blitz photograph showing the ruined St George's Church and to its right no. 4 St George's Street, the gown shop of François Eldonné. Rubble is still piled on the path and it is interesting to note that the wall of the church and iron railings survived the bombing. Beyond the church can just be seen the sign of the White Lion public house at no. 6. Although this photograph was taken soon after the 1 June raid the Censor did not allow it to be published until 29 June.

The Catholic Women's League provided this mobile canteen to assist the hundreds of rescue workers brought into the city after the blitz. This photograph shows the destruction in Burgate looking towards the Buttermarket, taken a few days after the raid and also shows some of the barrage balloons that arrived after the main event. In her book *Though the Streets Burn*, Catherine Williamson suggests that the balloons came up from Exeter, which was hit by German bombers a few weeks before.

Dr Hewlett Johnson , Dean of Canterbury, enjoying a cup of tea while talking to one of the soldiers engaged in the clear up operation in the precincts. Although some damage to property had been experienced in earlier raids the bombing of 1 June caused far more devastation. However, the Cathedral itself escaped largely unscathed with the only casualty being the library which suffered a direct hit. The library was subsequently rebuilt and opened in 1954.

Burgate Street and Iron Bar Lane viewed from Bell Harry Tower of the Cathedral soon after the blitz. St Thomas's Church and the tower of St Mary Magdalen were spared major damage but all around was devastated. The shell of Court Bros. store can be seen in Iron Bar Lane (previously Godden & Son's depository) as well as the walls of Austen's printing works adjacent to it. Nothing remains of the Crown Inn, which stood on the corner, apart from a lone chimney stack.

Members of Canterbury's Home Guard (No. 2 Platoon, A Company) in Westgate Gardens, October 1944. The platoon was part of the 3rd Battalion and includes Messrs D. Breeze, D. Prett, J. Newman, A. Percival, C. Redmond, A. Wiffen, P. Holmes, S. Holman, S. Parry, E. Potts, C. Anslow, D. Bean, H. McLean, F. Maple and S. Neaves. Formed in May 1940, the local Home Guard stood down from active service in October 1944 and a special recognition service was held at the Cathedral on 3 December 1944 following a march past through the city.

ARP personnel at the back of Orchard House, 173 Wincheap, early 1942. Apart from Mr Lye, who was in charge of the group, all the members were volunteers undertaking various roles from ambulance drivers to messenger boys. Those seen are, back row (left to right): Messrs Hinton ?, George Briggs, Fagg, Seymour, Hugh Mitchell, Douglas Lye, Don Beerling, 'Lofty' Hogben and Cyril Wood; front row: Ruth Taylor, Mrs Seymour, Reg Mitchell, Harry Lye, Percy Wilcox, Mr Todd, -?-. Orchard House, once a private school run by Miss Brothers, was destroyed in an air raid on 31 October 1942 when houses in neighbouring York Road were also hit. Fortunately the First Aid post was transferred elsewhere just a few days before the bombing. It is rather ironic that on 11 March 1939 Canterbury's MP Sir William Wayland, when talking about the ARP, said 'that some people in Canterbury thought the city could be a danger zone but this was not the case – certainly a town like Canterbury would never be made an objective'! The site of Orchard House is now occupied by Sladdens the heating engineers.

Part of the interior of the 'City' Printing Works of J.A. Jennings Ltd. in St George's Lane after the 1 June air raid. The works were completely gutted and a tangled mass of machinery and debris from the building are seen here. In the *Kentish Gazette* published on 6 June 1942 the firm were advertising their temporary printing works at Harbledown Place, Summer Hill with a reception office for enquiries at Goulden's shop in the High Street.

J.A. Jennings' Printing Works in St George's Lane looking towards Watling Street after the blitz. On the right-hand side of the photograph the ruins of St Mary Bredin Church can just be seen. The large building on the left was Salem House, the only property to survive on the western side of the lane. From the early years of the century until the late 1920s the *Kent Herald* (established in 1792) was published by J.A. Jennings. The firm was founded by John Adolphus Jennings and for a time was situated at 8 Guildhall Street, but had moved to 18 St George's Lane by the early 1890s.

A MISCELLANY

Sue and Geoffrey Daniel investigating the 'hermit caves' in the grounds of the old St Mary's Jesuit College at Hales Place, 1959. This photograph was taken by Mark Daniel long before the area was extensively developed for housing. Copinger Close was built on this site. The Jesuits left Hales Place in the mid-1920s and the buildings were demolished a few years later.

Part of the Canterbury Exhibition at St George's Street, summer 1951, the year of the Festival of Britain. Canterbury was chosen as one of the twenty festival cities and the exhibition ran from 11 June to 12 September. It showed the part that the city played in the history of the country from the Iron Age through to the post-war period and in particular the role played by Augustine in the spread of Christianity throughout the country.

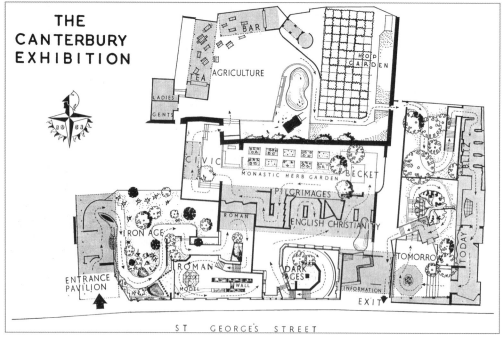

The plan of the Canterbury exhibition site located on the south side of St George's Street, 1951. After passing through the entrance pavilion visitors were reminded of the city's place in history through exhibits featuring the Iron Age, Roman Canterbury, Saxon Canterbury, English Christianity, Archbishop Thomas Becket, Pilgrimages, Monasticism, Civic Government, Agriculture and ending with the Blitz, Today and Tomorrow. As soon as the exhibition finished the site was prepared for redevelopment, nearly ten years after the blitz.

Stanley Jennings was elected Mayor of
Canterbury in May 1949 and served in that
capacity for the three years to 1952. He was
elected a member of the old city council after
the last war before becoming an Alderman and
serving as Sheriff in 1954. As Mayor in 1951 he
was particularly involved in arrangements for
the city's participation in the Festival of Britain
and set a fine example by helping to clear the
site in St George's Street. He was awarded the
OBE in the 1952 New Year's Honours in
recognition of his devoted service in connection
with the festival celebrations.

The Becket Courtyard in the Canterbury Festival Exhibition, 1951. In an area bounded by walls of the old
Whitefriars (adjoining the Simon Langton Boys' School) knights and churchmen kept watch where, rising
from the ground, a great pair of hands carried a model of the Cathedral and a sword, symbolizing the
balance of power between Church and State. I clearly remember going round the exhibition as well as
attending many of the other activities.

Walter Cozens, a local builder and archaeologist, a few years before his death in 1928 at the age of sixty-nine. The *Kentish Gazette* of 28 April 1928 reported that he 'early acquired a love of archaeology and there was scarcely a square inch of the historic city which he did not know'. Mr Cozens was largely responsible for the formation of the Archaeological Society in 1920 and became its Honorary Secretary in 1921. He also founded the Canterbury Art Society.

Alderman Harold Dawton blowing the city's ancient brass burghmote horn. He was the Sheriff in 1946 and Mayor in 1953 and 1954. Mr Dawton joined with Frank Amos to form the company Amos and Dawton, the city's longest established estate agency. Harold Dawton died in 1986 at the grand age of ninety-eight. Dating back to the days of the burghmote (the forerunner of a borough council), the horn was sounded to announce meetings and is still used on special civic occasions.

Michael Powell directs local boy Jimmy Tamsitt in a scene from the film *A Canterbury Tale* made in and around the city in 1943. Michael Powell, one of Britain's most brilliant film directors, was born at Howlett's Farm at Bekesbourne in 1905, moving a few years later to Hoath Farm in Bekesbourne Lane from where he rode to Canterbury by pony to attend the King's School. Jimmy, who lived in Fordwich, played a character called 'Terry' in the film, an experience he looked back on with great enjoyment and some pride. In November 1996, the actress Sheila Sim (Lady Attenborough) unveiled a plaque at Mr Powell's birthplace.

The Bourne family of Watling Street photographed in the Westgate Studio of C.W. Allen. Charles Allen, who lived at 1 Hanover Place (now Roper Road), was in business during the 1880s when this photograph (or 'cabinet card') was taken of a typical Victorian Family in the city. Mr Allen's studio had closed by the late 1880s when there were at least six photographers operating in the city.

This lance-corporal in the Buffs (East Kent Regiment) was photographed in J.G. Charlton's studio at Mercery Lane. It is possible that he is wearing the Queen's South Africa medal. John G. Charlton's first premises were at 54 St George's Street, but he moved to Mercery Lane at about the turn of the century becoming the cathedral's official photographer. He remained in business until after the Second World War.

A 'Cabinet card' by Arthur Francis Colbourne, photographer and artist. He had his studio at 58 St George's Street from about 1900, having previously had premises at 18 Castle Street. His advertisement on the back of this card reminded customers that he was 'under Royal and Distinguished Patronage' and mentioned that Christopher Marlowe was 'born on premises occupying this studio 1564'.

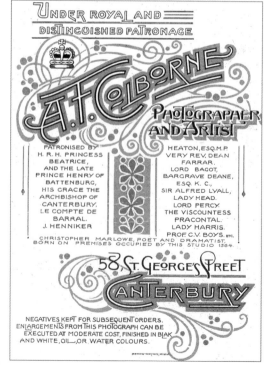

The motor ambulance purchased by the Kent and Canterbury Hospital in the early 1920s. The new vehicle (reg. no. FN 6061) is seen outside the old hospital at Longport. The *Kentish Gazette* of 20 October 1923 reported that 'it should be emphasised that in providing this motor ambulance the Hospital is supplying a service the cost of which, in the great majority of towns, is borne by the rates'.

This poster relating to recruits for the East Kent Militia was printed in 1807 and published as a postcard in 1904. The bounty of thirty guineas seems an attractive proposition, although it was not an easy life in the militia. The *Kentish Gazette* of 17 March 1794 reported that 'a court martial was held for three soldiers for wantonly breaking down the trees and otherwise damaging the plantations of the public walks in Danejohn field, who being found guilty were sentenced to receive 100 lashes each'.

ACKNOWLEDGEMENTS

A good number of local people have helped with this compilation but I am especially grateful to Monica and Reg Page, Reg and Hugh Mitchell, Tony Coe, Gerald Cramp and Bob Simmons for the loan of personal photographs and their assistance with particular aspects of the book. My thanks also go to the following for the loan of and/or permission to use a number of postcards and photographs:

Mary Baldock, Jim Beale, Bill Blackman, Tony Blake, Peter Bradley, Win Browning, Fred Chapman, Carole Clark, Margaret Coomber, Paul Crampton, Mark Daniel, Joan Davey, Robin Edmonds, Arthur Goodwin, Peggy Gordine, Maurice Hart, Stuart Heggie, Lou Howard, Patsy Kerr, Jimmy Long, Neil Mattingly, Dorothy May, Denis Reding, Nita and Eric Rigden, Maurice Spillett, Win Tamsitt, Joyce West, Harry West, Rob Williams, Peg Wilson, Tony Wright and Marjorie Young.

I owe a great deal of thanks to the very many people who have assisted me with information and as always to David Cousins and his fellow staff at the Canterbury Library for their courtesy and ready help. Once again I am grateful to the Kent Messenger Group Newspapers for permission to reproduce a number of *Kentish Gazette* photographs and last but not least to Jim Styles whose skill was severely tested in the copying of a variety of original photographs.

As with previous books, my thanks also go to my wife, Isabel, for typing the manuscripts and for her assistance in all aspects of this production.

BRITAIN IN OLD PHOTOGRAPHS